| DATE | | | |
|---|---|---|---|
|  |  |  |  |
|  |  |  |  |
|  |  |  |  |
|  |  |  |  |
|  |  |  |  |
|  |  |  |  |
|  |  |  |  |
|  |  |  |  |
|  |  |  |  |
|  |  |  |  |
|  |  |  |  |
|  |  |  |  |
|  |  |  |  |

# HOW TO DO YOUR OWN
# PROFESSIONAL
# PICTURE
# FRAMING

No. 1238
$11.95

# HOW TO DO YOUR OWN
# PROFESSIONAL
# PICTURE
# FRAMING

## by Raymond D. Brown

## TAB BOOKS Inc.
### BLUE RIDGE SUMMIT, PA. 17214

FIRST EDITION

FIRST PRINTING

MARCH 1981

Library of Congress Cataloging in Publication Data

Brown, Raymond D
    How to do your own professional picture framing.

    "# 1238"
    Includes index.
    1. Picture frames and framing.   I.   Title.
N8550.B76      749'm7      80-28145
ISBN 0-8306-9650-4
ISBN 0-8306-1238-6 (pbk.)

# Contents

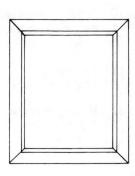

# Introduction

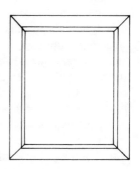

It seems that there has been a revival in crafts. Everywhere you go people are holding fairs, seminars and classes to show, teach and pass on their expertise to any willing soul who will listen. Crafts are performed by some people for pure relaxation. Others treat crafts as a way to make a living and get away from the eight-to-five world.

The reason why you choose a craft or hobby is not as important as the self-satisfaction you get from it. I recently designed and constructed a new bedroom suit for my little girl. She watched daily with great patience. When it was finally placed in her bedroom. I was repaid a thousand times for my labor with the delight she showed. Each time a visitor comes to the house, she wants to show them her bedroom. My daughter knows that it was made just for her, and her joy keeps compounding my satisfaction of doing something with my hands.

Picture framing is a craft which can be both rewarding and money saving. How many times have you visited a frame shop or gallery and and admired a frame you just could not afford? I am sure that situation has happened to you as it has to me. Not being able to afford something is often the only stimulus needed to get you interested in a craft. By framing your own pictures, you will save the labor costs charged by the professional framer or the factory which produces ready-made frames. It is true that you may have to purchase a few tools for framing, but if you are into woodworking you probably have the necessary tools. On the other hand, the frames you produce will save you an amount many times over the cost of the tools.

Another plus in favor of producing your own frames is the finish they need. By doing your own finishing, you are in complete control of the final result. In a later chapter you will receive some of the basic procedures with regard to finishing your frames. By learning to mix colors and not having a fear of experimentation, you should be able to finish a frame any way you choose. The long standing and popular wax and stained process of finishing is also included, and more than likely will often be used. Although there are many moldings on the market in a great array of finishes and colors, I feel that creating my own finishes is more exciting and rewarding than purchasing a finished molding.

A statement often heard is, "I could never do that." And my answer is, "sure you can." Yes, it does take a certain amount of skill, but doesn't everything that you have learned up to this point in your life? Mistakes will be made, but do things again and again until everything is right. I feel the word expert should be used very loosely in any discussion, or maybe not at all. What you learn from this book was in turn learned from other contacts, sources and through practice. Man learns by imitation and through communication. If you have a problem, never hesitate to seek the help of an established craftsman. Most craftsmen talk to and guide you through any problem you have.

The purpose of this book is to teach you to make your own picture frames. In the following chapters you will be led through the various steps of producing a picture frame. The basic procedures of framing should be followed until you feel you have the experience to go on your own. Feel free to experiment and have a positive attitude toward your work. Along the way, you will probably pick up some ideas of your own. When you in turn pass along those ideas, you will be the teacher. Happy framing!

Raymond D. Brown

# Moldings 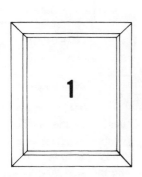 1

A *molding* is the boundary around a picture and is spoken of as the *frame* (Fig. 1-1). Although the molding is a vital part of the framing, it is but one of the many parts in a total framing job.

In early art, the painting was usually made on a board or boards glued together with the picture area scooped out to about ¼ inch in depth. The outside area that was left is the forerunner of our modern day frame. After a while the frame became separate, and two types of frames which evolved were the *platform* and *center panel*, which are still popular today (Figs. 1-2 and 1-3).

## TYPES OF MOLDINGS

The modern moldings of today come in many shapes and finishes for the craftsman. Figure 1-4, which shows the face, and Fig. 1-5, which illustrates the profiles and corners, are but a small sampling of the moldings on the market. Most lumber and building centers handle at least one brand of moldings in either the finished or unfinished variety. Also, many mail order houses handle a full range of moldings and supplies for the framer.

If you wish to build up your own profiles, you can purchase *builder's moldings* (Fig. 1-6). With builder's moldings, you must create the rabbet which holds the picture, but it is an easy operation as you will see. Many different arrangements or profiles can be made with the builder's molding if you simply use your imagination. Another plus to this type of molding is that you can finish the frame in any way you desire.

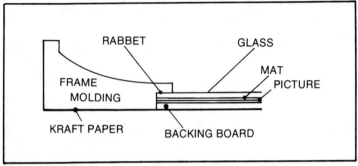

Fig. 1-1. The molding is one of the many parts of the framing.

Now that some of the different moldings have been seen, a question in the back of your mind is probably which frame should you use for certain works of art. The first and most important point to be made in selecting a molding is to never over frame a picture. The molding you choose, as stated earlier, is but one part of the total framing. The frame must be harmonious with the total composition and must not be more important in the composition and must not be more important in the composition than the picture itself.

## GUIDELINES FOR MATCHING MOLDINGS WITH PICTURES

When you place a piece of molding against a picture, if it is pleasing to your eye, you have probably made the right choice. The best solution to matching a molding with a picture is through experimentation, but a few general guidelines are as follows.

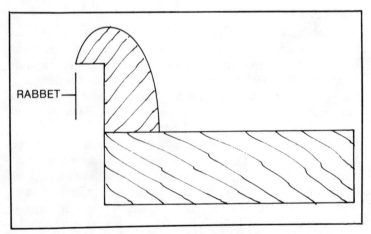

Fig. 1-2. The platform style is a flat with a raised edge.

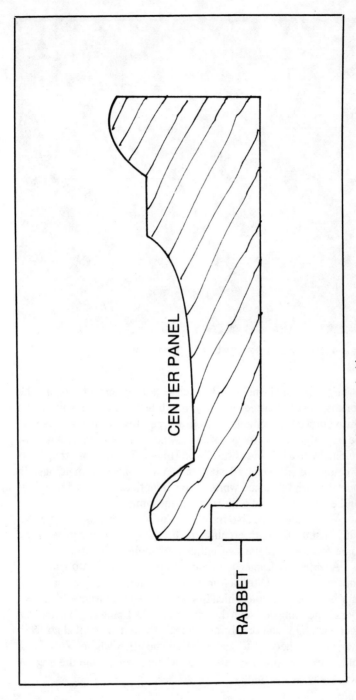

Fig. 1-3. The center panel style is a flat with a molding on each side.

11

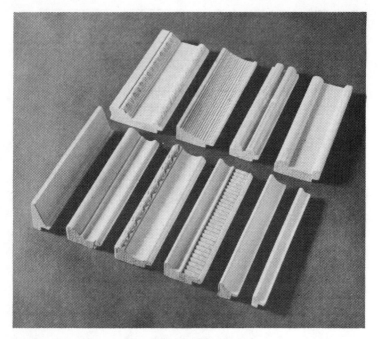

Fig. 1-4. The faces of moldings by Klise Manufacturing.

For black and white works such as *etchings* and *lithographs*, the work is usually matted, which you will learn later, in white or off white before the framing. With this type of work, glass is used in the framing process for protection. The frame is usually a narrow molding with a black or natural wood finish. Etchings or lithographs in color are also matted and framed with narrow moldings. In contrast with black and white, color in both the mat and moldings can be experimented with to your advantage.

Watercolors are also framed under glass, and usually a wider mat is used than with etchings or lithographs. The choice of the frame for a watercolor can either be simple or ornate.

A *canvas* is framed according to the category into which the work of art falls. Often a *liner* is used when framing a canvas. A liner is merely a frame which fits within the outer frame. The liner offers a blending between the canvas and the frame and is usually in a contrasting finish or fabric-covered. Even in a small abstract, a liner may be needed to make the composition whole. With large bold abstracts, you may only need a thin strip around the edge of the canvas as a frame.

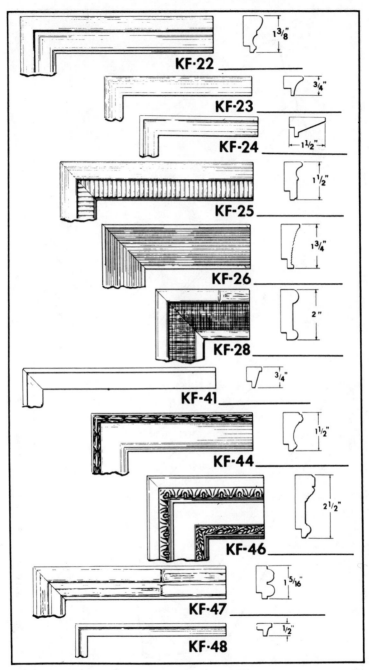

KF·22    1 3/8"

KF·23    3/4"

KF·24    1 1/2"

KF·25    1 1/2"

KF·26    1 3/4"

KF·28    2"

KF·41    3/4"

KF·44    1 1/2"

KF·46    2 1/2"

KF·47    1 5/16"

KF·48    1/2"

Fig. 1-5. The profiles and corners of various moldings.

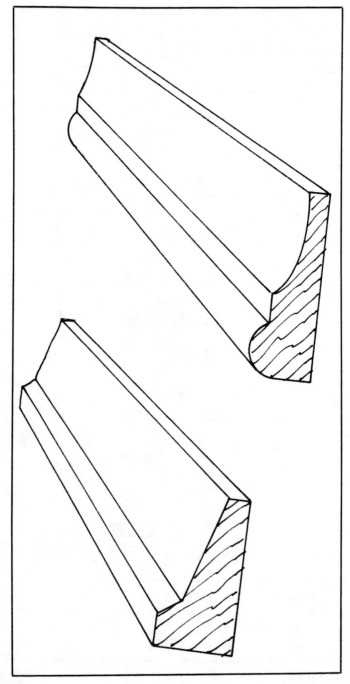

Fig. 1-6. Builder's moldings are common lumber yard items.

In the beginning you may need some help in trying to decide the weight of molding and finish to use on different works of art. One of the best suggestions is to visit a museum or muse through art books to get some advice. When you see a picture, make a mental note of the molding and finish. Some day you may be faced with the same situation.

If you now find yourself confused a little, it is only natural. Practice will develop your skill in choosing the proper molding. Always be on the lookout for other framers' solutions to their framing jobs.

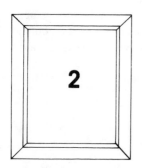

# 2 | Picture Framing Tools

As with any hobby or craft, there are certain tools or supplies you will need to purchase for your work. For picture framing, the outlay for tools is very small in comparison with other crafts or hobbies. Another good point to make is that picture framing can be done entirely with hand tools. Some, and maybe all, of the tools listed later may already be in your tool chest. Many of the tools are basic items for the craftsman.

If you already have power tools, you can use them in picture framing. There are many setups which lend themselves to framing. In a later chapter the use of power saws will be seen in making a molding from raw lumber. Check your manual or power tool handbooks at the library to get ideas which would benefit you in picture framing.

## MEASURING AND CUTTING TOOLS

The first step in framing is the measuring and marking of dimensions for the frame. The wooden *folding rule* and metal *tape measure* are the best tools for the job (Figs. 2-1A and 2-1B). The rule should be of good quality and easy to read. There are many different brand names on the market. When you choose, remember that the accuracy of measuring can not be overemphasized.

After the measuring and marking of the molding, the next step is to cut a perfect 45 degree angle. For this operation you will need a *miter box* and a *backsaw* (Figs. 2-2 and 2-3). Miter boxes come in a large assortment from the simple wooden box to special mitering

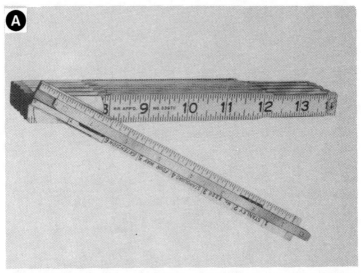

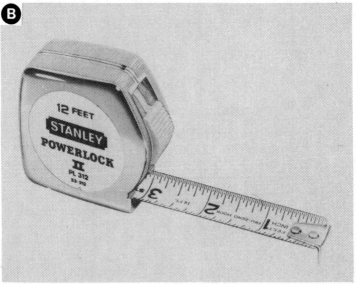

Fig. 2-1. Purchase a measuring device of good quality. (A) Wooden folding rule. (B) Metal tape measure.

machines. For the occasional frame, the wooden box can work just fine. If you intend to make a business of your framing, you may want to step up to a more sophisticated model. The backsaw is of equal importance in that it must make a clean, accurate cut. The impor-

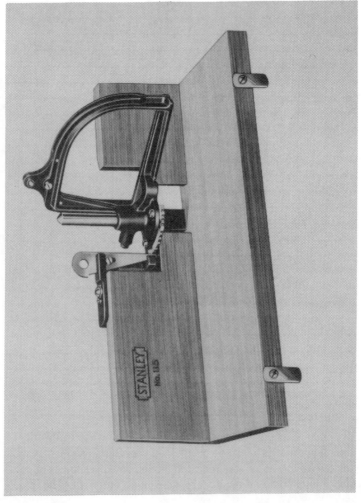

Fig. 2-2. This miter box is perfect for the beginner.

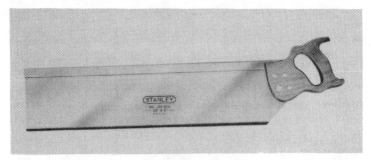

Fig. 2-3. The backsaw should be of high quality.

tant part of picking a saw is choosing one whose teeth will stay sharp and hold a good set. It is almost impossible to get a good clean cut with a dull saw. If the saw is constantly being returned to the sharpening shop, your money has been spent foolishly.

If your miter box does not have a hold-down clamp, it is wise to use *C-clamps* to hold the molding while it is being cut. C-clamps are a general item in hardware and building supply stores and come in an assortment of sizes (Fig. 2-4). When using the C-clamps, be

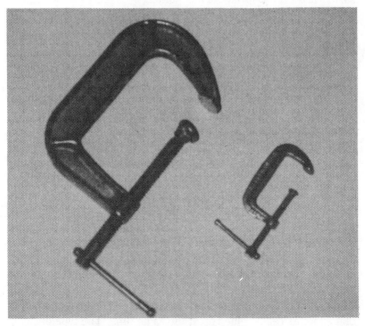

Fig. 2-4. C-clamps come in an assortment of sizes.

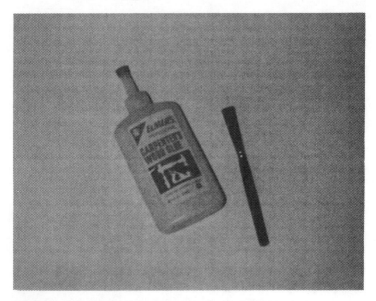

Fig. 2-5. A good glue and brush are important in joining.

sure to protect the surface of the molding by placing a wooden block between the molding and metal surface of the clamp.

## JOINING TOOLS

After the joints have been cut and lightly sanded, you are ready for the tools used in joining the molding. First, you will need a brush to remove any dust left by the cutting and sanding. The brush you use could be of the type used for painting. After the cut is clean, you will need to spread a thin bead of glue on the surface. Spread it about with a stiffer brush than the one used for dusting, to insure that the moldings will adhere. There are many glues on the market, and that choice is up to you, but the glue and brush in Fig. 2-5 do a fantastic job in the gluing operation.

Any joint needs to be put under pressure after it is glued for the glue to bind properly. For the holding operation you may wish to purchase a *vise* as in Fig. 2-6, which is a more expensive type and is used in a professional shop. As can be seen, the vise is of high quality and will accommodate about any size of molding you wish to work with. For a smaller investment, you can purchase the clamp as seen in Fig. 2-7, which can be purchased in sets of four in order that all joints can be glued up at the same time. The type of clamp shown can be attached to the top of your work bench with screws.

Fig. 2-6. This vise is used by the professional.

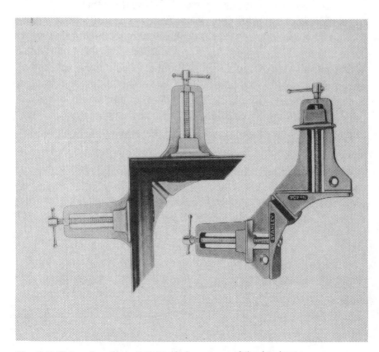

Fig. 2-7. This miter clamp is in the price range of the beginner.

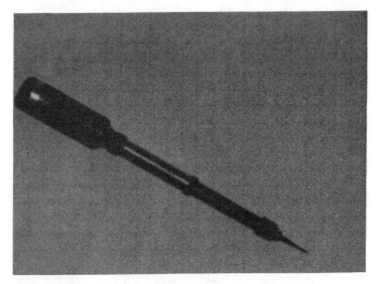

Fig. 2-8. A push drill is a must for drilling holes.

After the gluing operation is completed, the joints will need to be reinforced with *brads* or *nails*. Different sizes of brads or nails can be purchased at building or hardware stores, and a good assortment should be kept on hand for different sizes of moldings. When joining small moldings with brads, you may not find it necessary to drill pilot holes. With larger moldings and nails, a *push drill* is useful (Fig. 2-8). The push drill comes with an assortment of bits which should fill the need for any size of pilot holes you need to drill. The brads or nails must be driven into the molding.

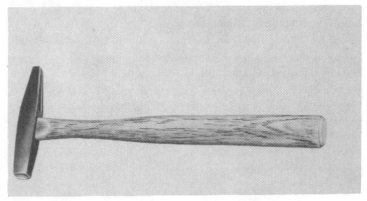

Fig. 2-9. The tack hammer can be used for driving brads.

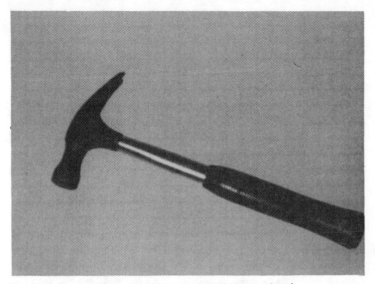

Fig. 2-10. Your hammer should feel comfortable in your hand.

For this operation your choice can run from the *tack hammer* to the 16 ounce *claw hammer* (Figs. 2-9 and 2-10). The choice of the hammer used should be made on whether or not it feels comfortable in your hand.

After the brads or nails have been driven, their heads will need to be set below the surface of the molding. The *nail set* is used for this operation (Fig. 2-11). Purchase a good quality nail set in the medium size range with a good flat point. When the nail is set, you will need to fill the hole with one of the fillers on the market. The list of fillers available is almost endless, but the one seen in Fig. 2-12 does a good job and has some very fine qualities. The filler shown comes in a dry powder form, which means you mix the

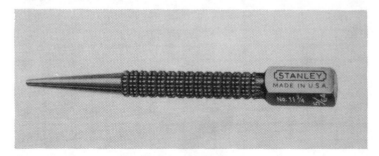

Fig. 2-11. The nail set should have a good flat point.

Fig. 2-12. This filler can be mixed as you need it.

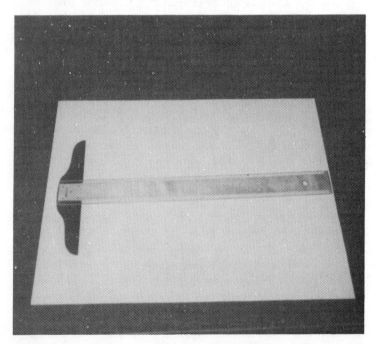

Fig. 2-13. The T-square enables you to lay out straight lines.

Fig. 2-14. The metal square cannot be nicked by the knife.

amount you need for the present job. The filler will mix with water or other finishing mediums according to directions. It sands well and finishes unseen.

## MATTING AND GLASS NEEDS

You will probably wish to mat most of your pictures, since matting adds so much to the total composition. You will need, in addition to the rule, a square, a *mat knife,* razor blades, a brush and *casein glue.* The *T-square* will aid you in laying out good straight lines on the mat (Fig. 2-13). If you are careful, you can use it as a guide when cutting on the line. A regular metal square can also be

Fig. 2-15. A sharp mat knife is a necessity.

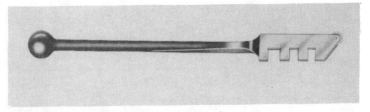

Fig. 2-16. A glass cutter is an inexpensive tool.

used for the same purpose, and there is no chance of the mat knife nicking the edge (Fig. 2-14). A good, sharp mat knife is a necessity (Fig. 2-15). Paper will dull your cutting edge faster than most materials, and the edge should be checked regularly for sharpness. The knife shown comes with extra blades which are stored in the handle. Replaceable blades are available. If you will be making mats which are covered, you will need the razor blades, brush and casein glue for this operation. The process used in covering mats will be discussed later.

Since you will wish to use glass in some of your frames, you will need to purchase the tool necessary for doing this job. The glass cutter is a very inexpensive tool and will last a long time if properly cared for (Fig. 2-16).

## TOOLS FOR FINISHING AND ASSEMBLY

For finishing your frame and final assembly, you will need a set of artists' colors (oils or acrylics), stain, shellac, artists' brushes, sandpaper, *steel wool*, wiping rags, *tack cloth* and wax. Most of these items you should have on hand if you have been doing any finishing. If not, they can be purchased at a paint or art store.

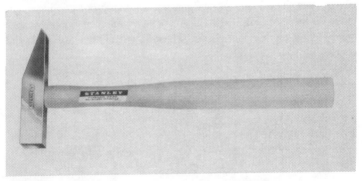

Fig. 2-17. A flat-sided hammer makes driving the brads easier.

For the final assembly you will need a flat-sided hammer to drive brads into the frame to hold the back on Fig. 2-17. Cardboard, kraft paper, an *awl* or *ice pick*, screw eyes and picture hanging wire are other required items.

This finishes your list of needed tools, which if purchased new would be of no great outlay of cash. The amount you spend on tools is in direct relation as to how far you want to go with your hobby of picture framing. Let's make a frame!

# 3

# Making a Frame From Picture Frame Molding

Now that you are educated in the materials and tools used in framing, it is time to do some actual practice. For this chapter you will build a frame to learn the mechanics of the different operations. After you learn the basics we are going into now, you should have the confidence to proceed to future chapters.

The first requirement is to find out how much molding you will need for the framing job. A simple formula is to add the length of the four sides of the picture to be framed to eight times the width of the molding used (which allows for the miter angle), plus about 2 inches for cutting allowance. Suppose the picture to be framed is 11 inches by 13 inches. For this picture size, you can figure 48 inches (total of sides) plus 16 inches (8 times the 2-inch molding used) plus 2 inches for the cutting allowance. The total length of molding needed would be 66 inches.

## TOLERANCE AND RABBET MEASURE

Before you start your measuring and marking of the frame size on the molding, a point needs to be made about *tolerance*. Tolerance in the frame size is needed to let you have an easy job of assembly when you start to insert the glass, picture, backing and such into the frame you have made. When framing a picture with the protection of glass, a 1/16-inch tolerance is needed on each side. For a canvas, a ⅛ inch tolerance is usually sufficient on each side. For your purposes, assume that the frame now being made will use glass and proceed as follows. If you allow the 1/16-inch

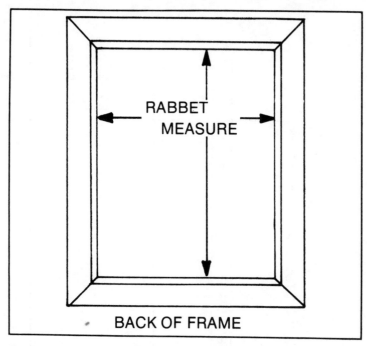

Fig. 3-1. The rabbet measure is the picture size plus tolerance.

tolerance, you will need to add ⅛ inch (the sum of two sides) to each measurement of the picture, which would give you the dimensions of 11 ⅛ inches by 13 ⅛ inches. From these measurements you have determined what is called the *rabbet measure* of the frame (Fig. 3-1).

After you have determined the rabbet measure of your frame, it is time to lay out the lengths of molding that you will need to complete the frame. You must remember that in laying out the lengths of molding, you need to allow for the miter on each end, which is equal to the width of the molding you use. In this framing practice you are using 2-inch molding, so to the rabbet measure of 11⅛ inches by 13⅛ inches you would add 4 inches or 2 times the width of the molding, as seen in Fig. 3-2. From these calculations, you should arrive at a short side which is 15⅛ inches and a long side which is 17⅛ inches. The best method of laying out and cutting your molding lengths is to do them one at a time and double check each measurement as you go. Your end result will be four pieces of molding, with two pieces being 15⅛ inches and two pieces being 17⅛ inches (Fig. 3-3).

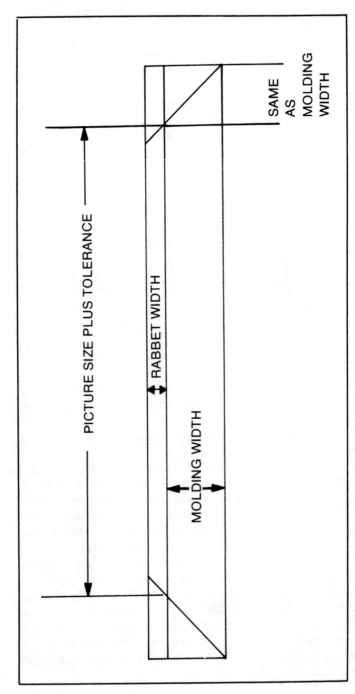

Fig. 3-2. Allow for the miter when cutting the molding to size.

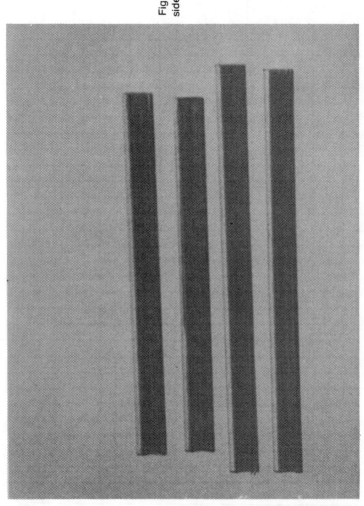

Fig. 3-3. Two short sides and two long sides will be needed for the frame.

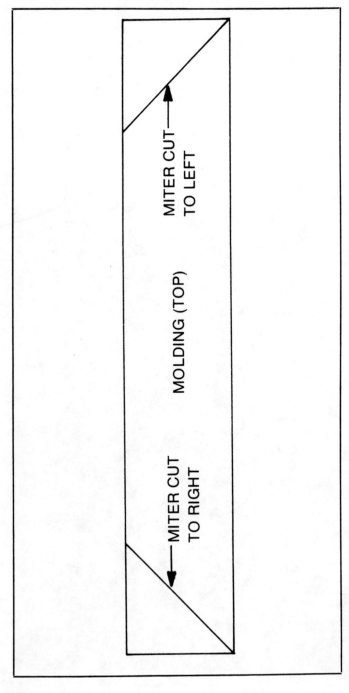

Fig. 3-4. Miter cuts are made in opposite directions.

## MAKING MITER CUTS

You are now ready to cut the miters in each end of the molding in the direction shown in Fig. 3-4. Align the end of the molding with the 45 degree slit as seen. Make the miter cut in one direction, holding the molding firmly by hand or C-clamps. A good miter cut cannot be over emphasized. Be sure that the molding is flat in the box, or you will make an angle cut which will never join up properly. After the miter cut is made in one direction, make the cut on the other end by using the 45 degree slit in the opposite direction (Fig. 3-5). After all ends of the molding are properly cut, smooth them by light sanding. You are ready for the joining of the frame.

## JOINING PROCEDURE

In preparation for joining you will need the four pieces of molding, a clamp or set of clamps, glue, a brush, brads or nails, a hammer and a nail set. If you are using a set of clamps, you can glue and nail the joints all at once. If you choose to use a single clamp, you will need to allow plenty of drying time before the joint is removed from the clamp. The choice is up to the individual and is in

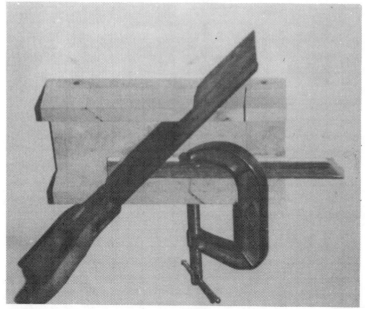

Fig. 3-5. The placement of the saw to cut the miters.

Fig. 3-6. Lay the four pieces of molding on the table as they would be when joined.

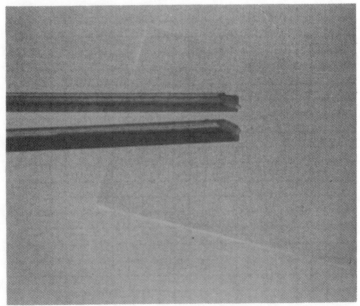

Fig. 3-7. A good bead of glue is necessary for joining.

34

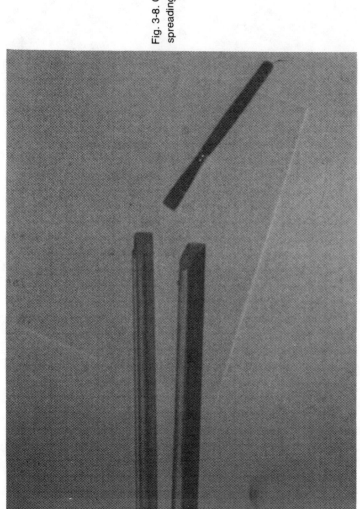

Fig. 3-8. Cover the entire gluing surface by spreading the glue with the brush

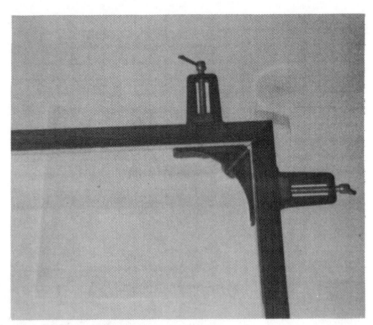

Fig. 3-9. Place the joint in the corner clamp to apply pressure.

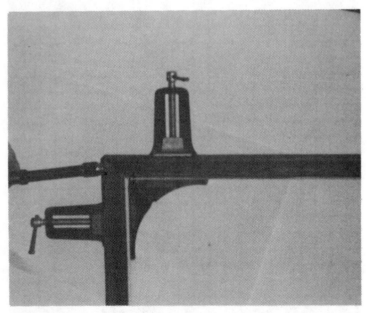

Fig. 3-10. Use the push drill to drill pilot holes.

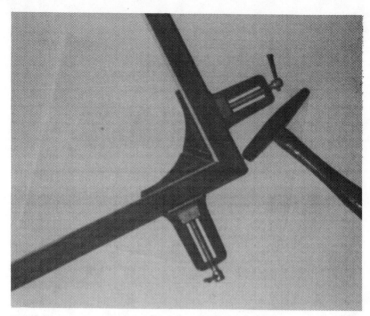

Fig. 3-11. Use the hammer to drive the nails in the molding.

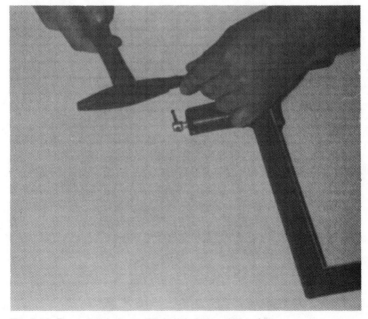

Fig. 3-12. The nail set places the heads below the surface.

relation to the amount of time you have to spend on your joining job. The important thing is to make a good clean joint by using the following steps.

Lay the four pieces of molding on your table as they would be when joined (Fig. 3-6). Start the joining by taking a long and short side and applying a good bead of glue to each cut (Fig. 3-7). Then spread the glue with the brush, covering the entire gluing surface (Fig. 3-8). When the glue has been spread, place the joint in the clamp, and tighten and allow proper drying time for the glue used (Fig. 3-9).

Do not remove the joined corner from the clamp, for the next step is to reinforce the joint with nails or brads. Start preparing the corners for nailing by drilling pilot holes, using the push drill, with a correct bit size which is slightly smaller in diameter and shorter than the nail or brad you will be using (Fig. 3-10). After the holes are drilled, drive the nails or brads as in Fig. 3-11. Next you will need the nail set to drive the heads of the nails below the surface (Fig. 3-12). When you feel the joint is properly dry and secure, remove it from the clamp and repeat the steps on each corner until all four corners are completed and the frame is done and ready for finishing (Fig. 3-13).

Fig. 3-13. The completed frame is ready for finishing.

Fig. 3-14. Fill the nail holes with putty.

If you used a finished molding for your frame, you will only need to fill your nail holes with a color matched putty (Fig. 3-14). Sand the area smooth. If you used an unfinished molding, fill the nail holes with putty and sand smooth. Directions for different finishes will be found in Chapter 5.

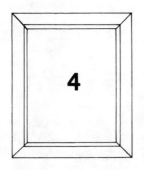

# Making a Frame From Builder's Molding

**4**

The use of builder's moldings in making picture frames is very popular for two reasons (Fig. 4-1). The first is that you can save a great amount of money by creating your own profiles, and the second is that you can apply any method of finish that you choose. The first reason probably attracts more people, but the second reason is also a very important consideration since you will learn finishing techniques in a later chapter.

When you work with builder's moldings, you will have to create a rabbet into which your picture can fit. A popular piece of molding used to perform the rabbet operation is called the *parting strip*, and measures ¾ inch by ½ inch, as seen in Fig. 4-2. The best method of joining the parting strip is by using the common *butt joint*. There is no need for the use of a *miter joint* for the rabbet strip, since it will be covered by a top molding.

## CONSTRUCTING THE INSERT

The first frame you should build is the insert as seen in the profile (Fig. 4-3). The insert is used as the inner frame which goes next to the picture, and may be used with a mat for prints or used in the same manner as a mat when framing a canvas. An insert is often called a liner when it is used in framing a canvas.

The first step in constructing your insert is to get an accurate measurement of the work you are to frame. Include in that measurement the tolerance for easy assembly as discussed in Chapter 3.

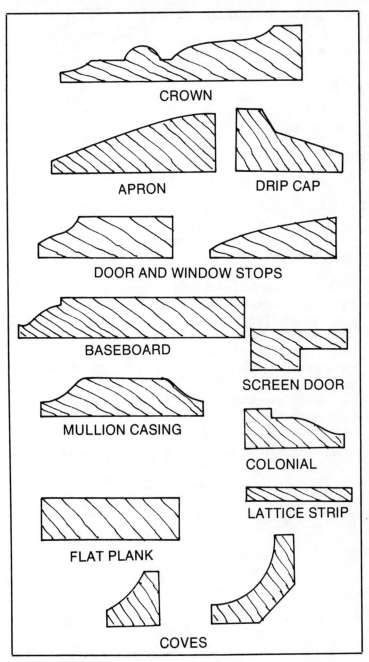

CROWN

APRON

DRIP CAP

DOOR AND WINDOW STOPS

BASEBOARD

SCREEN DOOR

MULLION CASING

COLONIAL

LATTICE STRIP

FLAT PLANK

COVES

Fig. 4-1. Builder's moldings come in many profiles.

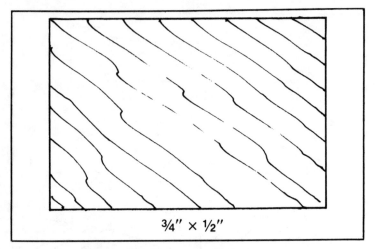

3/4" × 1/2"

Fig. 4-2. A strip must be added to form a rabbet.

Never take it for granted that the material you are to work with is perfectly square. The first step you often need to make is to square the material by making a 90 degree cut with your miter box (Fig. 4-4). After the end has been cut square, you are ready to measure and cut the sides of the rabbet strip. Remember that the long sides will overlap the short sides, so take this into consideration.

After all measurements have been calculated and checked, start by measuring a short side as in Fig. 4-5, making ready your first cut. After the measurement, place the strip in your miter box

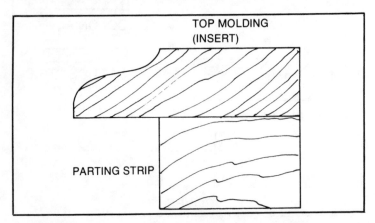

TOP MOLDING
(INSERT)

PARTING STRIP

Fig. 4-3. Attach the strip to the molding with glue, brads or both.

and make your cut at 90 degrees as shown (Fig. 4-6). Make sure the saw cut stays on the waste side of the strip. You now have your first short side cut. The best method of getting the opposite side the same length is shown in Fig. 4-7. Place the first piece next to the remaining strip, making sure the ends are flush, and take your measurement from the first cut as seen. This method is by far better than measuring each strip with your tape. After the second short side is laid out, cut it at 90 degrees as you did with the first side. You now have your two short sides made and are ready to lay out the measurements for the long sides, as seen in Fig. 4-8. Make your cuts as you did on the short sides until you have four strips, ready for joining (Fig. 4-9).

The method of joining will be as with any molding—glue and brads. Start the joining by applying glue to the end of a short side (Fig. 4-10). Then place the short side and long side in your gluing clamp as in Fig. 4-11, and tighten and let the glue dry. The use of brads will help to reinforce your butt joint. Use two brads on each corner by placing one brad near the top and outside, and the other brad near the bottom and inside (Figs. 4-12 and 4-13). This method of placing the brads will keep the strip from twisting. Follow the steps until all four corners have been joined, and your rabbet strip will be complete. Your next step will be to prepare the top molding of the insert.

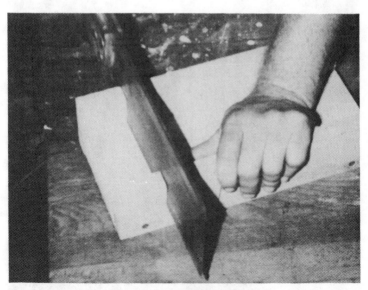

Fig. 4-4. Make a 90 degree cut with your miter box.

Fig. 4-5. Lay out your measurements on the molding.

Fig. 4-6. The molding is placed in the miter box for cutting.

Fig. 4-7. Take your measurement from the first cut.

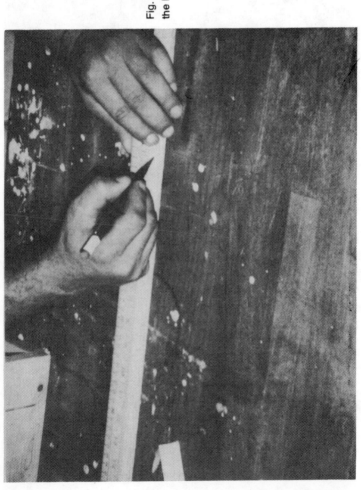

Fig. 4-8. Laying out the measurements for the long sides.

Fig. 4-9. The four strips are ready for joining.

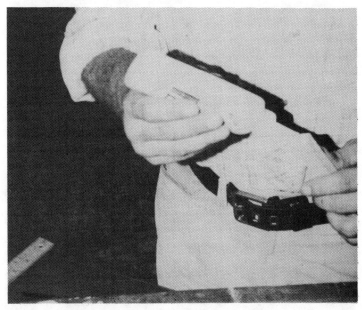

Fig. 4-10. Apply glue to the end of a short side.

47

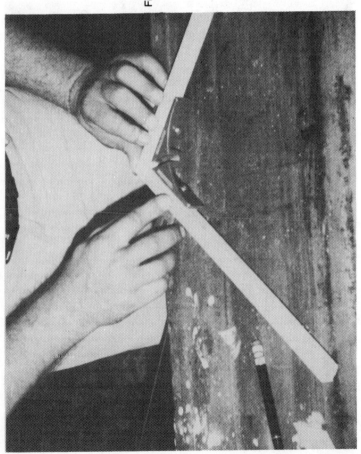

Fig. 4-11. Tighten the clamp to let the glue dry.

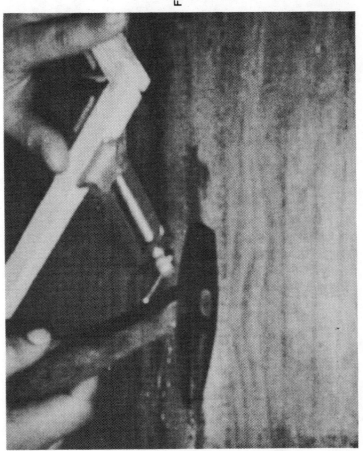

Fig. 4-12. Brads help to reinforce your butt joint.

49

Fig. 4-13. Proper brad placement will keep the strip from twisting.

## PREPARING THE INSERT'S TOP MOLDING

The top molding will have corners which are mitered. The first step is to make sure you have a square end to work from, as you did with the rabbet strip. Since the sides of the top molding will be the same length as your parting strip frame, you can choose two methods of measuring. One is seen in Fig. 4-14. Measure the parting strip frame and transfer that measurement to the back of your molding. Also, you can place the molding next to the parting strip frame and mark the dimensions (Fig. 4-15). Either method you choose will work fine. After the dimensions have been laid out, make your first cut as in Fig. 4-16, and the second cut as in Fig. 4-17, being sure the cuts are made in the opposite direction of one another. After the first piece of molding is cut, place it next to the remaining material and transfer the measurement to insure accuracy as you did with the parting strip. Continue the above steps until all four sides have been made and ready for joining.

As with the parting strip frame, you should use glue and brads in your joining operation. First, take a short side and apply glue to one cut end. Place it in your gluing clamp along with a long side. Tighten the clamp and let the glue dry. Your next step is to reinforce the joint with brads. Drill pilot holes if you feel the

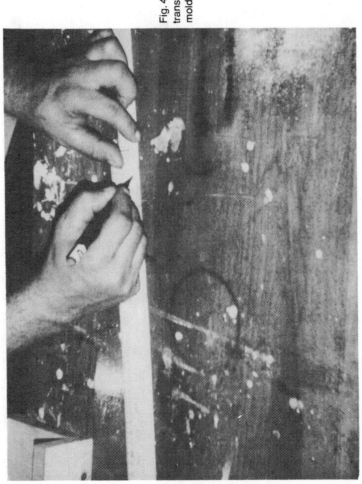

Fig. 4-14. Measure the parting strip frame and transfer that measurement to the back of the molding.

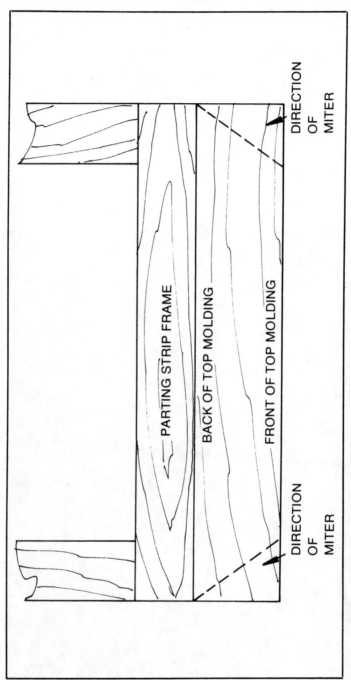

Fig. 4-15. You can place the molding next to the parting strip frame and mark the dimensions.

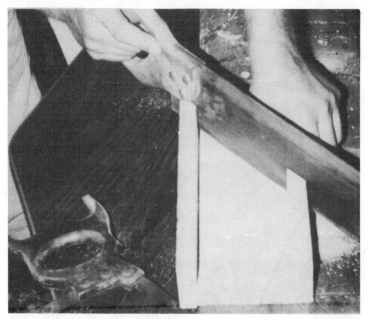

Fig. 4-16. Making the first cut.

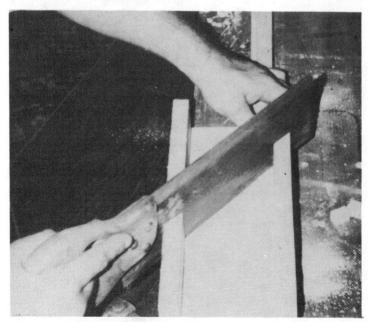

Fig. 4-17. Making the second cut.

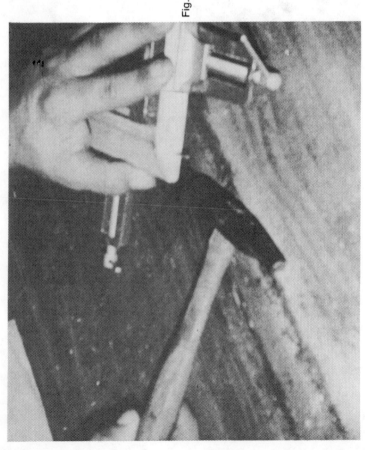

Fig. 4-18. Drive a brad near the inside on one side.

molding could split while driving the brad. If not, continue by driving a brad near the inside on one side, and near the outside on the opposite side (Figs. 4-18 and 4-19). Continue until all four corners are joined in this manner. There is no need to set the nail heads on the insert since it will be covered by the outer frame.

After the top molding has been joined, apply glue to the parting strip frame (Fig. 4-20) and attach to the back of the top molding with the aid of short brads (Fig. 4-21). Let the entire assembly dry. You are now ready to measure your insert and make your calculations for your top frame (Fig. 4-22). The insert which you just finished will fit into a rabbet, again made from parting strip and attached to the back of the outer molding. Make this rabbet strip in the same manner you did on the rabbet strip for the insert. Instead of the picture to be framed setting the dimensions, you will take your measurements from the insert as in Fig. 4-22. For your tolerance, make an allowance as you would for a canvas to give yourself plenty of room for assembly. If the insert is a loose fit, you can insert cardboard wedges between the insert and rabbet to tighten it up. After the second rabbet frame has been prepared, you are ready to construct the top outer frame, which is the last part of your complete frame.

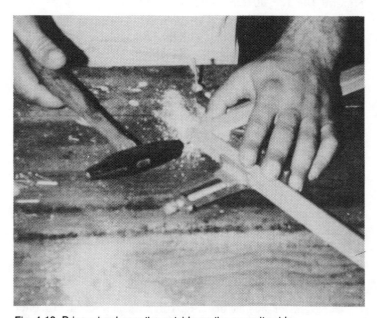

Fig. 4-19. Drive a brad near the outside on the opposite side.

Fig. 4-20. Apply glue to the parting strip frame.

## MAKING THE TOP OUTER FRAME

Since the size of the outer frame is the same as the sides of the rabbet strip, lay your molding with the back next to the side of the rabbet strip frame. Transfer the dimensions in a direct manner as you did with the insert. After the measurements have been made, make your first cut in the molding and your second end cut in the opposite direction (Fig. 4-23). After the first piece of molding has been cut, make a cut in your material in the direction shown in Fig. 4-24. By using this method, you have one end of your next piece cut. You can stand it next to the first side and transfer the measurement directly to insure accuracy (Fig. 4-25). After one set of sides has been made, measure and cut the other two sides in the same fashion. You are ready to join your frame.

As with the insert, you will need to use glue in your joining, but instead of brads you will probably need to use finishing nails. The size of the nails will be in direct relation to the size of molding used. Before nailing, drill pilot holes. The first step in joining your outer frame is to apply glue to the end surface of a short side and long side (Fig. 4-26). Place the sides in your gluing clamp. Tighten the clamp and let the glue dry (Fig. 4-27). As mentioned, drill pilot holes for the nails before driving. Drive the nails as with the insert,

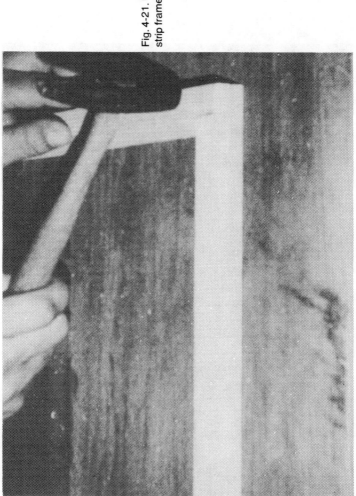

Fig. 4-21. Use short brads to attach the parting strip frame to the back of the top molding.

57

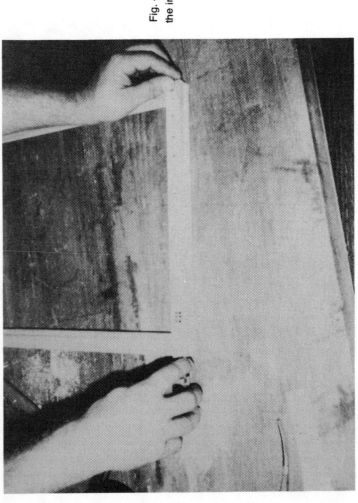

Fig. 4-22. Take your measurements from the insert.

58

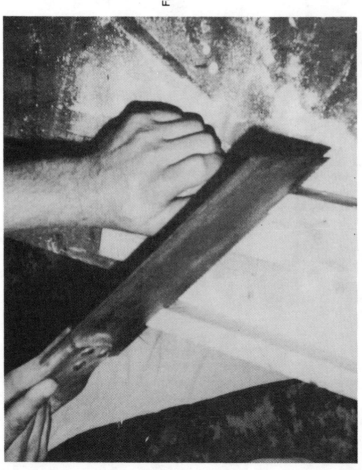

Fig. 4-23. Make your first cut in the molding.

Fig. 4-24. Make a cut in the direction shown.

Fig. 4-25. Transfer the measurement carefully.

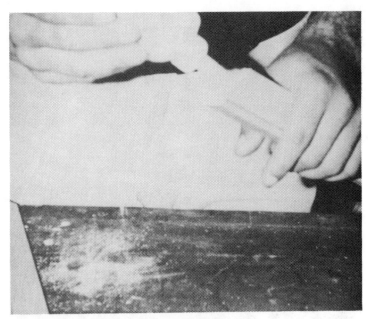

Fig. 4-26. Apply glue to the end surface of a short side.

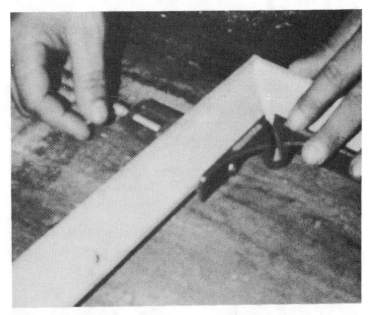

Fig. 4-27. Place the sides in a clamp.

Fig. 4-28. Drive the nails. Place one near the inside and one near the outside on the opposite side.

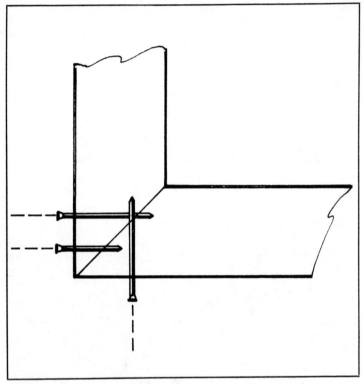

Fig. 4-29. You may need to use three nails for heavy moldings.

placing one near the inside and one near the outside on the opposite side (Fig. 4-28). For a heavy molding, you may need to use three nails as in Fig. 4-29. Continue to join each corner until the frame is complete (Fig. 4-30). The next step is to attach the rabbet strip to the back of your molding as you did with the insert—with glue and brads. After the rabbet strip has been attached, give the glue time to dry. Then set the nail heads below the surface (Fig. 4-31). Your frame is ready to be finished.

## COMBINATIONS

The frame you have just made is but one of the many different combinations you can achieve with builder's moldings. It is worth your time to make a visit to your local lumber yard to see the many different profiles they have on hand.

In Fig. 4-32 you see a baseboard molding used in combination with a *mullion casing* molding, with the rabbet being formed with a

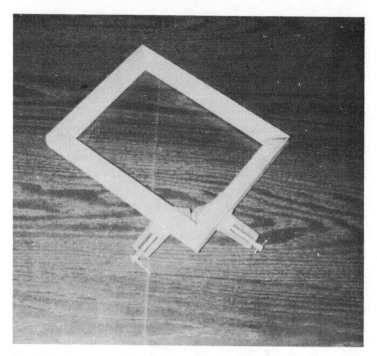

Fig. 4-30. Join each corner until the frame is complete.

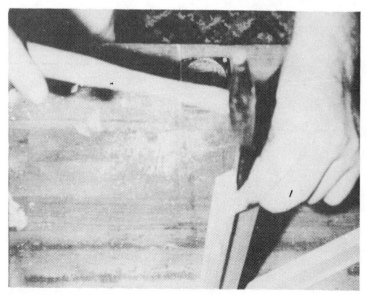

Fig. 4-31. Set the nail heads below the surface.

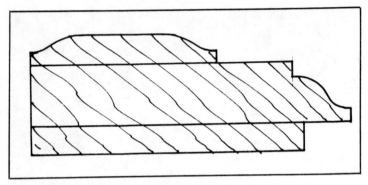

Fig. 4-32. A baseboard and mullion casing combination.

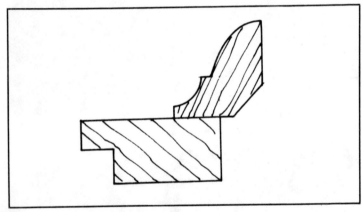

Fig. 4-33. The combination of a screen door molding and bed molding.

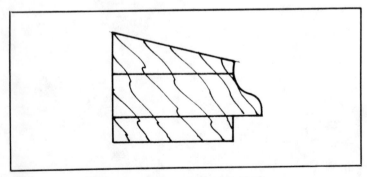

Fig. 4-34. Two window and doorstop moldings stacked.

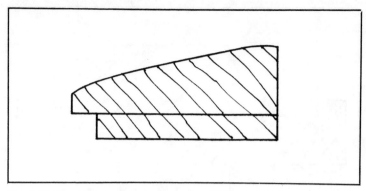

Fig. 4-35. The apron molding has a gentle slope.

lattice strip or any flat plank to a desired thickness. In Fig. 4-33, a *screen door* molding is used in combination with a bed mold. This combination produces a very nice frame. It is made by attaching the bed mold on top of the screen door molding with glue, brads or both.

Another good combination is made by using two *window* and *doorstop* moldings, stacked one on the other with a lattice strip forming a rabbet (Fig. 4-34). If you wish a simple frame with a gentle slope, you may consider the *apron* molding in combination with a lattice strip or flat plank to form a rabbet (Fig. 4-35).

If a wider frame is needed, you can turn to a *baseboard* or *crown* molding. These are two nice moldings by themselves, and the baseboard molding can further be enhanced by a bead molding (Fig.

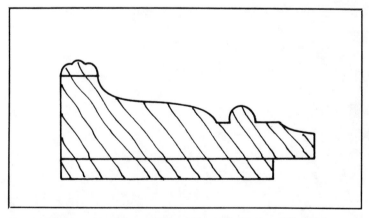

Fig. 4-36. The baseboard or crown molding makes a nice wide frame.

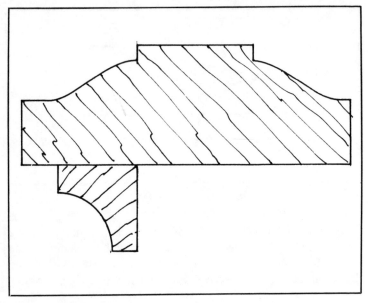

Fig. 4-37. The mullion and cove combination can be used for a shadow box.

4-36). If a deep rabbet is needed as in constructing a shadow box, one combination is the *mullion casing* and *cove* molding (Fig. 4-37).

# Finishing 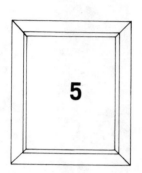 5

Finishing your frame in the proper manner is as important as the construction of the frame. Good finishing will not cover a poor job of assembly, but it will make the project worthwhile if carried out properly. The different methods of finishing are many, and you are sure to find some of your own after you have experimented with the basic methods which will follow. The amount of time you spend on getting a good finish will be paid for in the satisfaction you will receive from this part of the framing operation.

It is best to start with an elementary approach to finishing by first learning to work with a wax over bare wood finish and a wax over stain finish. The supplies you will need for these two finishes will include an assortment of regular penetrating wood stains, shellac, a good quality brush for the shellac, a supply of soft, line-free wiping rags, sandpaper, steel wool and a good grade of wax.

## WAX AND STAIN FINISHES

The first finish you should try is the simple wax finish. This is a finish which works well with quality woods such as oak and walnut. With the wax finish it is important that a good piece of wood has been chosen for the molding. Check the molding for any blemishes, and sand the molding smooth with extra fine sandpaper. It is very important that you have a surface that is entirely smooth to get a fine finish. To get an even smoother surface for your finish, you will need to rub the surface with extra fine steel wool, and then

Fig. 5-1. A waxed finish is beautiful on hardwood.

wipe the surface clean with a *tack rag*. The tack rag should remove any dust which is on the surface of the molding. But keep checking and wiping until you feel that your finished surface is dust free. When you are satisfied with the surface, apply a light coat of white shellac, thinned with a little alcohol. If you want your wood to have a darker tone, add a little orange shellac to the white. When the shellac has dried, your next step is to rub the surface with extra fine steel wool. Although the rubbing will tend to dull the finish, its sheen will return when you apply the wax. A paste wax is used for the final coating. It is applied with a clean soft rag, given time to dry properly, and then buffed with a clean soft rag until a satiny gloss is achieved as in Fig. 5-1.

If you desire a stained finish for your frames, the following instructions will guide you in getting a professional finish. As with the waxed finish, the first important step is to provide a smooth surface upon which to apply the finish. Sand, steel wool, and wipe the surface as you did with the waxed finish before applying the stain. The first step is to apply the stain with a brush or rag to the surface of the molding, and wipe off any excess with a soft rag. Some of the stain will remain heavier in crevices or carvings which can add to the finish. Give the stain proper drying time. Then apply a thin even coat of shellac. After the shellac has dried, rub the surface with extra fine steel wool until a smooth finish is achieved. You are now ready to apply the wax, as with the waxed finish, by applying and buffing the surface to a smooth sheen, as seen in Fig. 5-2.

## COLOR BASICS

If you plan to use colors in your finishing, there are some basics to colors and color mixing you should know. Bright, flashy colors may work for a child's room where the decorating scheme has a cartoon effect. In general framing, though, you will need to use a toned down color so that your frame will not be more important than the picture you are framing.

If you have had any art courses, you are probably familiar with the *color wheel* (Fig. 5-3). If not, this information could be valuable for many different crafts. As seen on the color wheel, there are three *primary* colors: red, yellow and blue. You can make any color by mixing the primaries. The *secondary* colors are the first example of mixing. The secondaries fall midway between the primaries. When you mix red and yellow, you will get orange. For green, the yellow and blue are mixed. Violet is arrived at by mixing blue and

Fig. 5-2. The stain and wax finish would serve many types of framing.

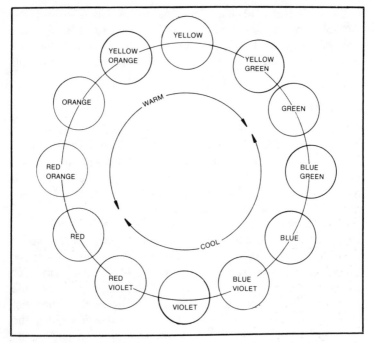

Fig. 5-3. The color wheel.

red. The *intermediates* fall between a primary and a secondary color. The intermediates include: yellow green, blue green, blue violet, red violet, red orange and yellow orange.

The color wheel is divided into two parts which are called *warm* and *cool* colors. The colors which contain a greater proportion of red or yellow are considered warm colors, and those colors having a greater degree of blue are the cool colors. The difference between warm and cool colors is that the warm colors appear to advance while the cool colors recede.

In the study of colors, you have probably run across the words *hue, value, chroma* and *tint*. Hue refers to the characteristic of a color which identifies it by a name such as red, blue, green, etc. The value of a color refers to the lightness or darkness of a color. The low values are dark and the high values are light, as can be seen by observing the color wheel and noticing that the colors become lower in value as they progress from yellow (the lightest value) to violet (the darkest value) at the bottom of the wheel. The chroma represents the degree of intensity of a hue. As a color is grayed or neutralized, its chroma is decreased. You can reduce the chroma of a color by the addition of a neutral gray or by mixing the color with its complement. Complementary colors are those which are directly opposite each other on the color wheel; red is the complement of green. By either method, you will not be changing the hue but merely the intensity of the color. Tinting changes the value of a color. To get a higher value, you add white to full strength colors. In instances when you wish to darken a color, you can either add a deeper value of the basic color to that you wish to darken, or mix the color with its complementary color.

## THE MIXING OF GRAYS

Cool and warm grays are often mixed and used in color finishes as an undercoat or as a top wash coat. When a gray is used as the undercoat, it is a usual practice to rub down the top coat of finish with steel wool when dry or rub with a soft rag while it is wet to expose part of the gray undercoat. As a top coat, the gray is thinned and brushed on. Then it is wiped off to mute a color such as red. Experimentation with the grays on scrap pieces and in conjunction with colors and stains will help you later in choosing a finish for your frames.

Fig. 5-4. Pour the white finish into a jar.

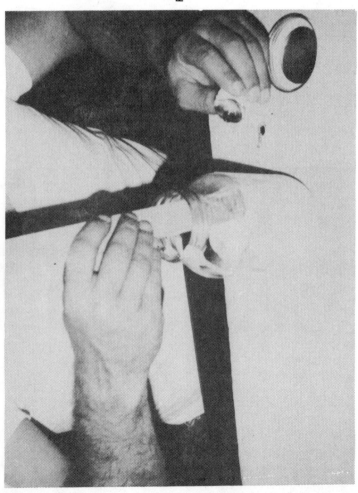

Fig. 5-5. Add the black finish.

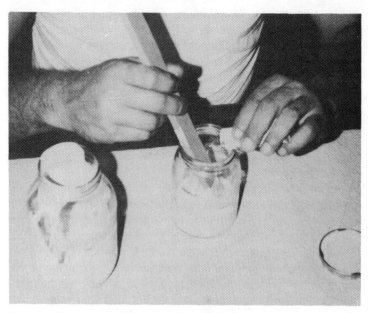

Fig. 5-6. Add a little blue to the neutral gray to make a cool gray.

The mixing of your grays is a simple operation with very few steps. First you must make a basic of neutral gray by adding a black to a white. Start by pouring the white into a jar (Fig. 5-4). Then add the black from a tube until the neutral gray is reached (Fig. 5-5). Stir the mixture thoroughly and add the black in small amounts, stirring constantly. What you want to achieve is a gray which falls at the midpoint of the scale. If you do not add enough black, your mixture will be too white. With too much black the mixture will tend to go toward a charcoal, which is too dark. A little practice is needed in mixing the neutral gray. The key to getting the mixture correct is to add the black in small amounts.

After you mix your neutral gray, you are ready to make a cool gray by adding a little blue to the neutral gray (Fig. 5-6). A warm gray is achieved in the same manner, but by the addition of a warm color such as a red or orange from the tube and then stirring (Fig. 5-7).

## SOME COLOR FINISHES

In finish one, the basic color is yellow with a white lip and an umber rubbed on and off the finish to create an antique look. The first step is to prepare the surface for finishing by careful sanding and wiping until a clean surface is made. After the surface is prepared, coat the entire surface with the cool gray you mixed. Acrylics will dry quickly but oils take time to dry, so allow plenty of time between each application. Apply a coat of yellow over the frame but not the lip. Paint the lip white. After the yellow and white have dried, you are ready to apply the top coat of umber. A thinned down umber is used by mixing the umber with water or turpentine according to the tube of paint used. After proper thinning, brush a coat of umber over the entire frame and wipe part of the umber off before it comes dry. The antiquing tones down the yellow into a much softer color.

Finish two is basically the same finish with a different color being used. In this finish red is used instead of yellow, and the lip is still painted white. The steps to follow are the same as in number one.

Finish three uses a different method of antiquing. Start this finish by sanding and wiping the surface clean. Paint the entire frame with a warm gray. Then apply a coat of red over the gray, covering the entire frame, including the lip. After the red has dried, the antique finish is completed by using a thinned cool gray as you did with the umber in finishes one and two. Brush on the cool gray and wipe the surface with a clean rag before the gray dries. This method also tones down the red and gives a different finish than when the umber was used.

Finish four uses the cool color of green with an antique finish. Sand and wipe the surface. Then apply a cool gray over the entire frame. Next, paint the lip of the frame with gold and the rest of the frame with green. After this has dried, brush on the thinned umber and wipe it off before it becomes dry.

Finish five also uses a cool color which is blue, with the lip being white. After sanding and preparing the surface, coat the entire frame with the warm gray you mixed. After the gray has dried, paint the lip white and the remainder of the frame blue. For this finish, a cool gray is thinned and used for antiquing. Brush on the gray and wipe as in the other finishes.

In finish six you will use the basic steps as the above finishes, but shellac is introduced into the steps of finishing. After preparing the surface by sanding and wiping, coat the frame with red and let it dry. A coat of gold is applied over the red and allowed to dry. Take a fine steel wool and rub down the gold until the red is exposed in places. Next apply a thin coat of shellac and allow it to dry. When the shellac has dried, a thinned warm gray is brushed on and wiped off the surface for the antiquing.

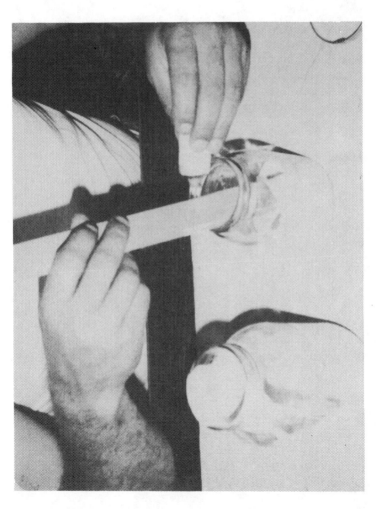

Fig. 5-7. To get a warm gray, you need to add red or orange.

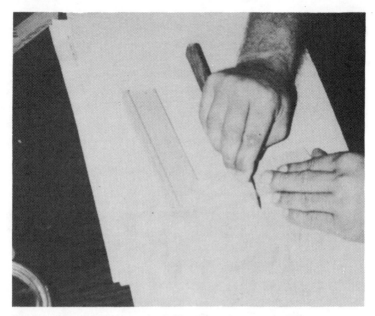

Fig. 5-8. A steak knife is used to add texture to an outside edge.

## ADDING TEXTURE TO YOUR FINISHES

A frame can often be enhanced by the use of texture on its surface. The important part of adding texture is to not add so much that it takes away the importance of the picture being framed. Two methods of texturing which will be discussed are scratching or marring the surface and a method of coating the surface with *gesso*, which is similar to a thick paint, and adding texture to that surface.

To distress or mar the surface, many regular household utensils may be used. In Fig. 5-8, a steak knife is being used to add texture to an outside edge. This method creates ridges and valleys which will show up differently when the finish is applied. Another utensil which may be used is a fork, which can make a texture on the surface in relation to the amount of pressure you wish to apply (Fig. 5-9).

The use of gesso as mentioned earlier in texturing was a practice often used on many of the older frames. The first step in the use of gesso is to brush it on the surface, building up a coat sufficient to hold a texture (Fig. 5-10). When the gesso is partially dry, usually after 15 minutes, you are ready to add the texture. A comb is often used to texture gesso. The gesso must be set up enough to hold the pattern of the comb's teeth without filling up the

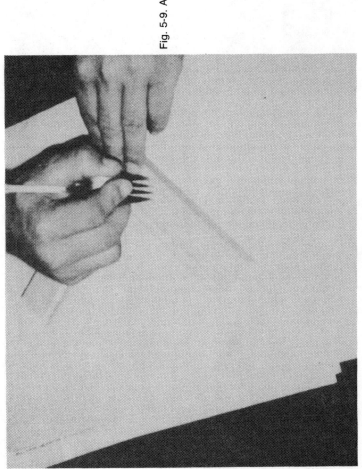

Fig. 5-9. A fork can also be used to produce texture.

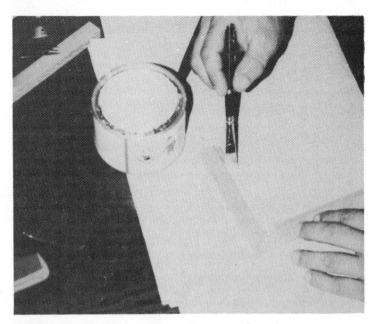

Fig. 5-10. Brush the gesso on the surface.

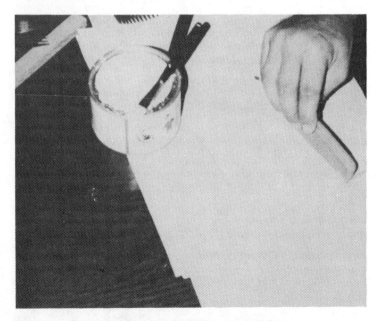

Fig. 5-11. You can add texture to the surface by combing.

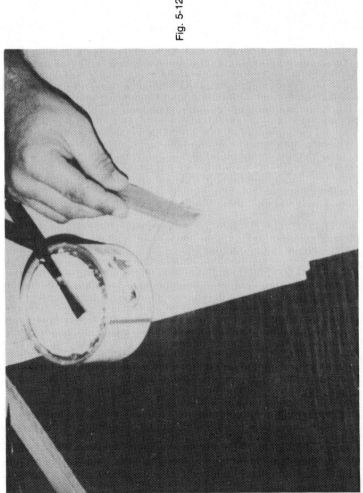

Fig. 5-12. Comb at an angle to add texture.

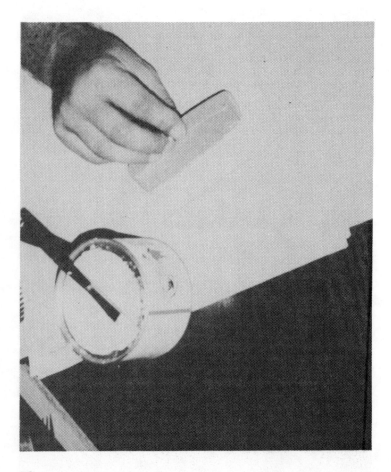

Fig. 5-13. The lip of the molding can also be textured by combing straight down.

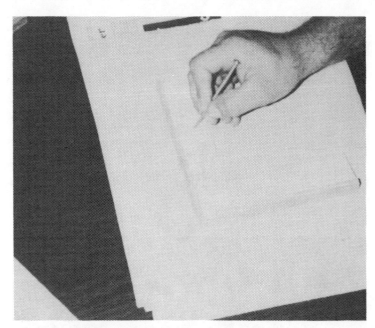

Fig. 5-14. Use a nail to scratch a design into the surface.

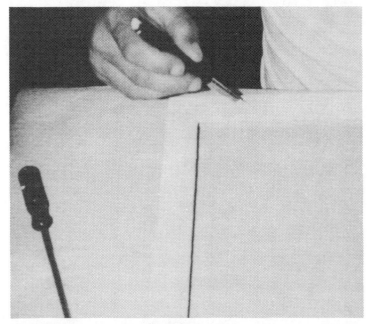

Fig. 5-15. Brush gesso on the lip of the insert.

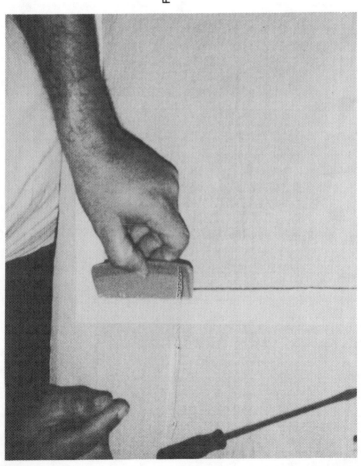

Fig. 5-16. Use the comb to add texture.

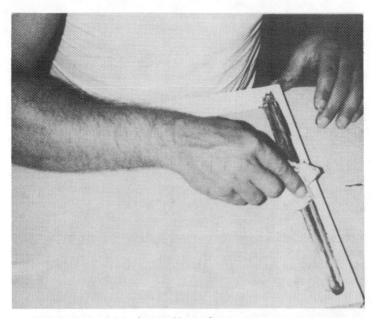

Fig. 5-17. Apply the finished coat with a soft rag.

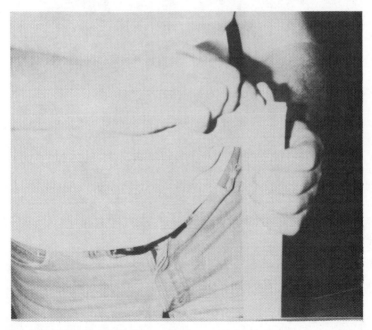

Fig. 5-18. Filling the nail holes.

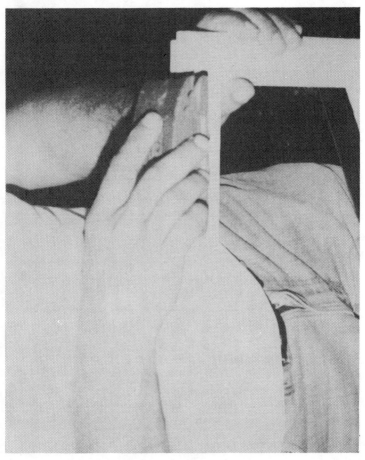

Fig. 5-19. Sand smooth.

Fig. 5-20. Distress the outside ridge with a steak knife.

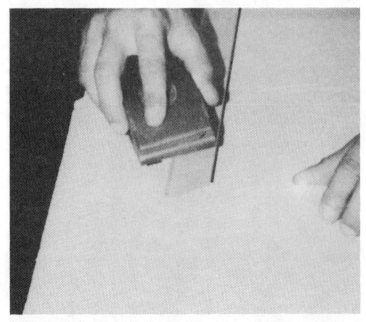

Fig. 5-21. Eliminate burrs by sanding.

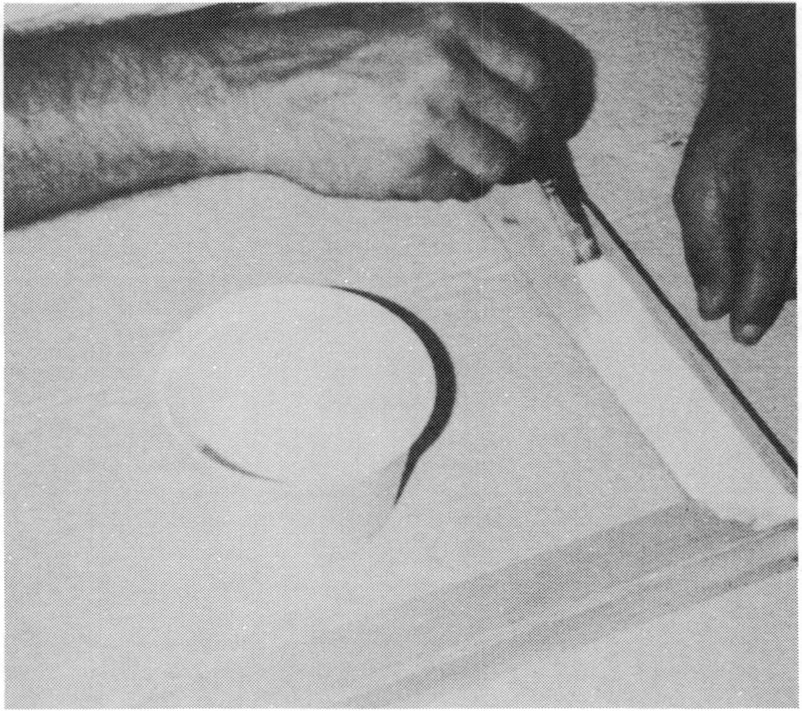

Fig. 5-22. Apply a coat of the warm gray to the surface.

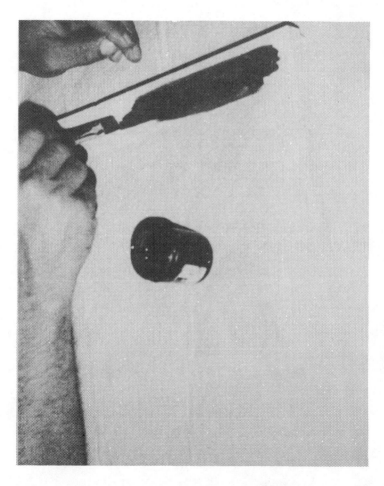

Fig. 5-23. Brush on a coat of stain.

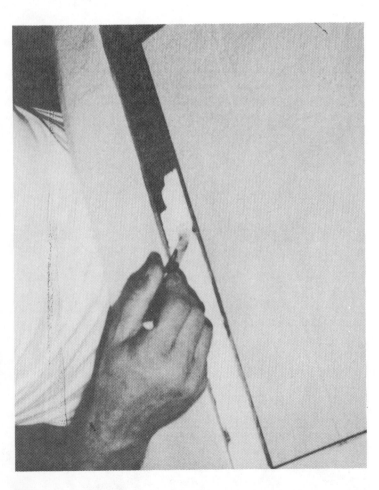

Fig. 5-24. Apply a coat of cool gray.

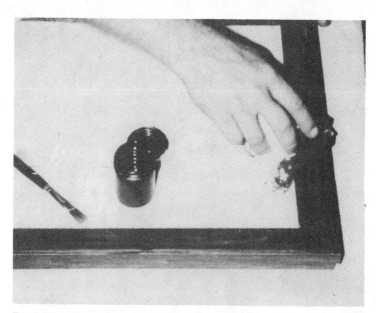

Fig. 5-25. Apply another coat of stain with a rag.

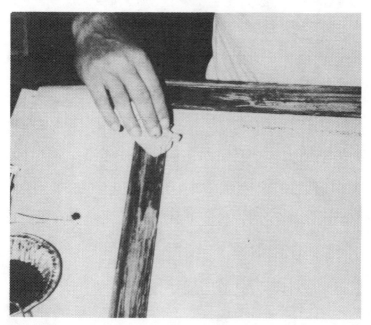

Fig. 5-26. Use a dry rag for wiping.

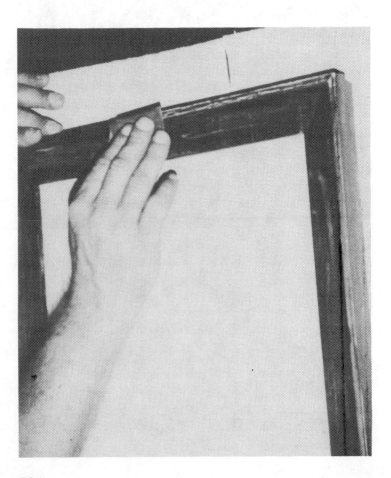

Fig. 5-27. Sand the outside ridge with sandpaper or steel wool.

92

valleys the teeth make when passed over the surface. You should experiment with different timing to get good results.

After the gesso has set, you can add texture to the surface by combing as in Fig. 5-11 or at an angle as in Fig. 5-12. The lip of the molding can also be textured as in Fig 5-13, by combing straight down or working at an angle. If straight lines are not wanted, you may wish to experiment with a wavy or swirling pattern.

Often a design is scratched in the flat surface of a molding. One method of achieving this form of finish is to apply the gesso in layers until you get a good built up surface of layers. The gesso may then be sanded to a smooth finish. A design can be scratched into the surface with a nail as in Fig. 5-14. To see how the steps mentioned are used in finishing, we will go through the finishing of the frame made in Chapter 4.

## FINISHING A FRAME

Start by brushing gesso on the lip of the insert you made (Fig. 5-15). When the gesso has set properly, use the comb to add your texture (Fig. 5-16). The next step is to add the finish coat which could be a color or, as in this instance, a walnut stain. As in Fig.

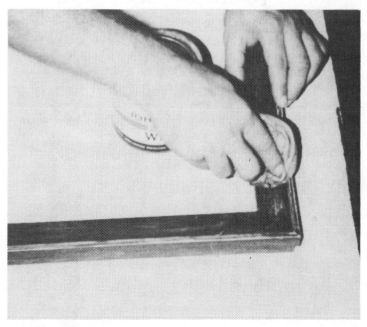

Fig. 5-28. Apply wax with a soft rag.

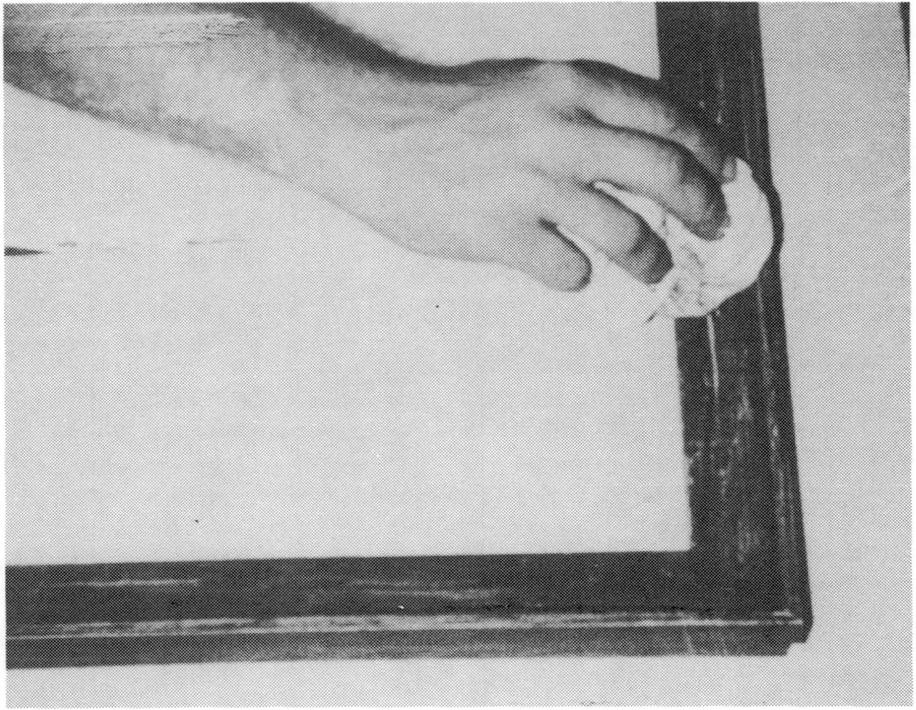

Fig. 5-29. Buff with another soft rag.

5-17, apply the finish coat with a soft rag by wiping it on the textured surface. Now set the insert aside to dry and turn to the finishing of the outer frame.

The first step in finishing the outer frame is to fill the nail holes (Fig. 5-18). Then sand smooth (Fig. 5-19). Next, distress the outside ridge with a steak knife (Fig. 5-20). The steak knife may create a few burrs. These can be eliminated by a light sanding as in Fig. 5-21. Coat the surface with a coat of the warm gray you mixed earlier (Fig. 5-22). When the warm gray is dry, brush on a coat of color or stain (Fig. 5-23). When this application is dry, work over the surface with a fine steel wool to expose the warm gray in spots. Next apply a cool gray and let this application dry (Fig. 5-24). Now another coat of color or stain is applied with a rag and then wiped with a dry rag while the surface is still wet to allow the grays to show through (Figs. 5-25 and 5-26). Take a fine sandpaper or steel wool and lightly sand the outside ridge to expose the finish under the stain (Fig. 5-27).

After the frame is dry, you are ready to apply wax to the surface. Apply the wax with a soft rag (Fig. 5-28). Then buff with another soft rag until a *luster* to your liking is achieved (Fig. 5-29). Your frame is now finished and ready to be assembled.

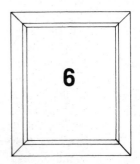

# 6 Mats for Picture Framing

A mat is like a cardboard frame around the picture. It allows for a break between the frame and the picture and prevents the work of art from coming into contact with the glass. The mat can make the total composition more pleasing, whether it is a mat in white, a color or one covered with material. Proportion is the important part of selecting a mat as well as color. The mat should not be the total focal point of the framing, but should be in harmony with the frame and the picture, both in size and color.

## MAT MEASUREMENTS

There are two important points to make about the size of mats. The mat border should never be the same size as the molding you use for the frame, and the bottom border should be a little larger than the top border. One method of arriving at a proper mat border size is the place the picture on a piece of matboard and move a piece of molding toward and from the picture until a satisfactory border size is reached.

After you have reached a proper border size for your mat, you are ready to lay out and cut the mat to the proper dimensions you have determined. Let's assume that you have arrived at a mat border size of 3 inches on the sides, 3 inches on the top and 3½ inches on the bottom. For this particular example, assume the picture will be a vertical hanging with the width of the picture or print being 14 inches and the height being 18 inches. The window of the mat, which will be laid out and cut later, should be ¼ inch

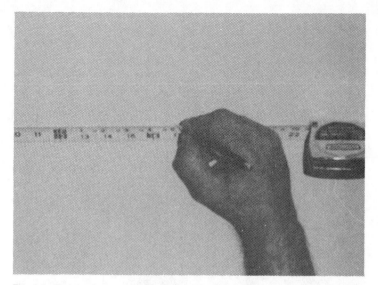

Fig. 6-1. The measurements are laid out on the mat.

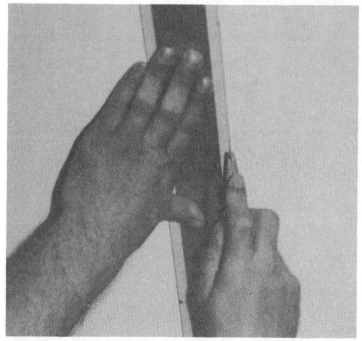

Fig. 6-2. Mat cutting requires a clean, flat surface, a sharp knife and a straightedge.

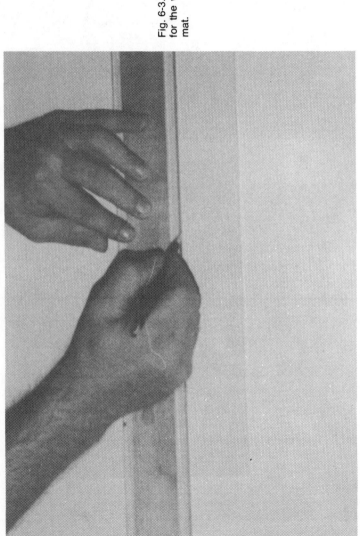

Fig. 6-3. Lay out the measurements for the window on the back of the mat.

smaller than the picture size to allow for an ⅛-inch lap on all sides to keep the edges of the picture from showing. You must take this into consideration at this point to get an overall measurement of the mat. Lay out the measurement for the height first. You know that the picture is 18 inches in height, so to this you add the total of the top and bottom borders, or 6½ inches. From this figure of 24½ inches, you must subtract ¼ inch, which is the overlap of the border, giving you a total height of 24¼ inches. The width is arrived at in the same manner by taking the width the picture, 14 inches, and adding the total of the side borders, 6 inches. Then subtract the ¼-inch overlap to arrive at a figure of 19¾ inches. Now you know the size of full measurements of the mat, and these measurements should be laid out on the matboard, as you get ready for cutting (Fig. 6-1).

## MAT CUTTING

For mat cutting, you will need a clean level surface to work on and a straightedge and mat knife to do the cutting (Fig. 6-2). Align the straightedge to the inside of the pencil line and make the first cut with steady but light pressure. You do not have to go through the matboard on the first cut, but instead you are scoring on the line to make the second cut. Make the second cut which should penetrate the matboard. Align the straightedge for the second measure-

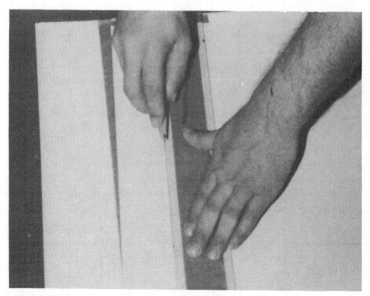

Fig. 6-4. Cutting out the window of the mat.

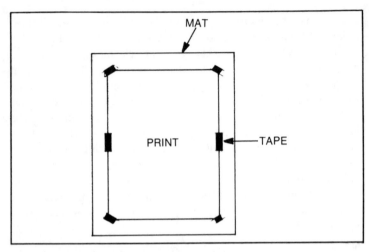

Fig. 6-5. The print is fastened at the center and corners.

ment and make the cut in the same manner as the first. You now have the outside dimensions of the mat laid out and cut. You are now ready to lay out and cut the window.

## WORKING ON THE WINDOW

Since there is a danger of your pencil lines overlapping and marring the face of the mat, it is best to lay the mat face down to lay

Fig. 6-6. Cut the material 2 inches larger than the mat.

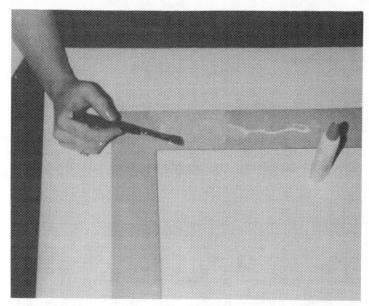

Fig. 6-7. Coat the face of the mat with glue.

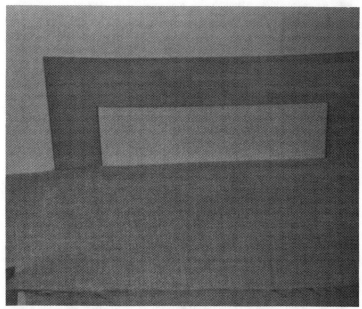

Fig. 6-8. Position the cloth on the face of the mat and keep it as straight as possible.

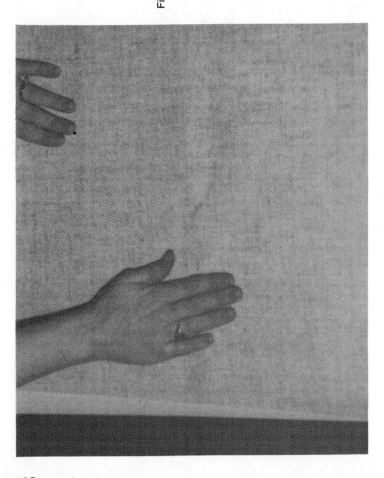

Fig. 6-9. Work out any bubbles in the surface.

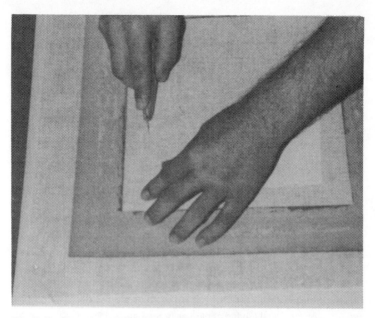

Fig. 6-10. Cut out the center of the cloth for the window.

Fig. 6-11. Make miter cuts to aid in folding the cloth over the edge.

Fig. 6-12. Apply a 1-inch band of glue all around the window.

out the window size. Lay out the borders according to the measurements you have calculated (Fig. 6-3). Use the straightedge and mat knife as before to cut the window out (Fig. 6-4).

You are now ready to mount the print or picture in the window opening by centering and taping it to the back of the matboard, fastening the print with tape at the corners and the center of the sides as shown (Fig. 6-5). You now have a finished matting. The size of your frame will now be controlled by the size of the mat as will be seen later.

As discussed earlier, mats are sometimes covered with a fabric such as linen or burlap in off-white or colors to give a different approach to matting. These materials can be found at most fabric shops and are sold by the yard.

## MAKING A COVERED MAT

To make a covered mat, start by making your mat as discussed before. Cut your material 2 inches wider than the size of the mat (Fig. 6-6). Now place the mat face up, and coat the surface with a casein glue all the way to the edge (Fig. 6-7). The glue should be spread thinly and evenly. After the glue becomes tacky, position the fabric over the mat, keeping it as straight as possible (Fig. 6-8).

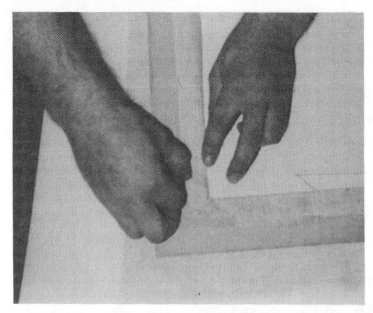

Fig. 6-13. Fold the cloth over and smooth out any bubbles.

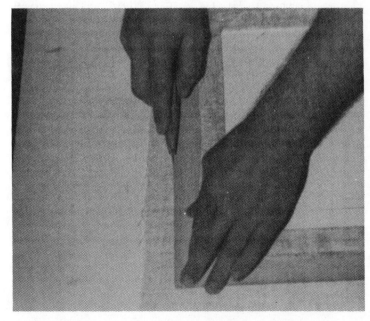

Fig. 6-14. Trim the edge of the cloth even with the edge of the mat.

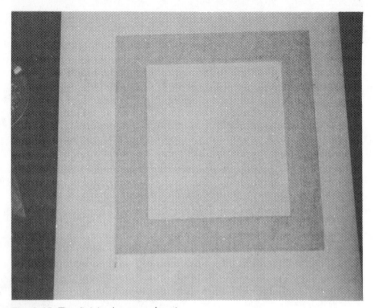

Fig. 6-15. The finished, covered mat.

You should work for a good adherence to the mat by starting at the center and rubbing to the edge as shown (Fig. 6-9). This step will work any bubbles out and give you a smooth surface. Next, turn the mat face down and cut out the center, leaving about 1 inch of the cloth to lap over the edge of the mat (Fig. 6-10). Make miter cuts in the material as in Fig. 6-11, starting near the edge of the matboard and cutting to the edge of the cloth. Apply a 1-inch band of glue on the back of the mat (Fig. 6-12). Fold the cloth over, and rub the surface smooth as before (Fig. 6-13). Trim the outside of the cloth to the edge of the matboard (Fig. 6-14). You have a finished mat as in Fig. 6-15.

# Glass Cutting 7

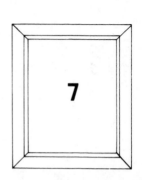

If you are going to frame watercolors, pastels or prints, you will need to give them added protection with glass. Glass adds depth to the medium as well as giving a finishing touch to the entire composition. Picture glass is usually used instead of regular window glass because it is thinner and clearer, but if it is not available the single strength window glass can be used. A non-glare glass is also available, but it is more expensive and will dim light colors because of its opaque quality.

## TOOLS FOR GLASS CUTTING

If you want to cut the glass yourself, the operation is fairly simple and tools needed are inexpensive. For glass cutting you will need a glass cutter, a soft lead pencil, a rule, a straightedge, and a little kerosene or oil to store your cutter in to keep the wheel in good cutting order. The surface upon which the glass is to be cut must be firm and smooth. A cardboard or carpet covered table will be ideal for the cutting operation. When the work surface has been prepared, you are ready to start your cutting operation.

## PROPER TECHNIQUE

The measurements for your glass must first be laid out with a tape and the soft lead pencil. Lay out your measurements carefully. Then lay your straightedge on the glass to start your cut (Fig. 7-1). When cutting glass you are merely scoring the surface, so be sure

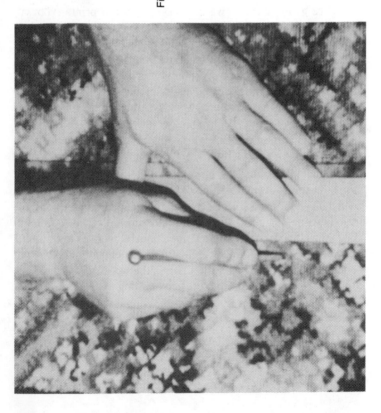

Fig. 7-1. Lay the straightedge on the glass to start the cut.

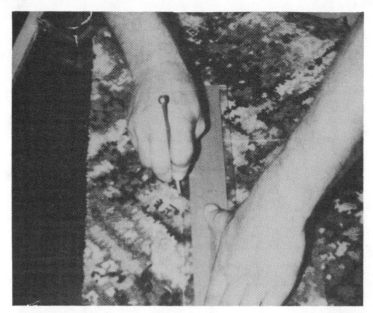

Fig. 7-2. Continue the cut across the glass.

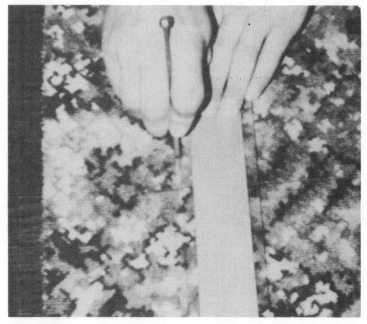

Fig. 7-3. Hold the cutter as shown.

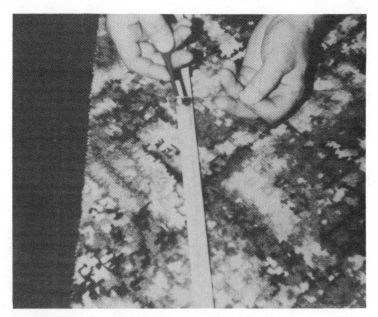

Fig. 7-4. Tap underneath to help the glass break off.

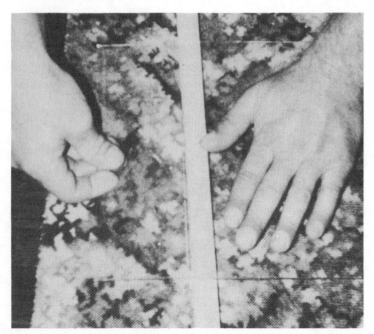

Fig. 7-5. Place a piece of wood under the scored line.

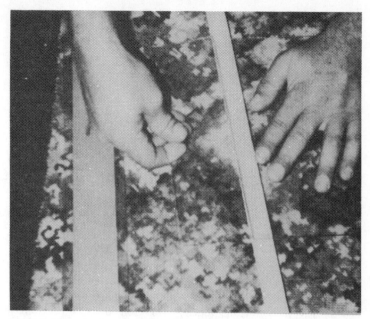
Fig. 7-6. The proper way to break the glass.

not to press too hard with the glass cutter. A firm constant pressure is needed for the scoring of the glass. When properly applied, the scoring action will sound much like that of cloth ripping. Start your cut on the far side of the glass as in Fig. 7-1, holding the cutter as shown. Continue your cut across the glass until you reach the near side (Figs. 7-2 and 7-3). After you have scored the glass along the line, it often helps to tap on the underneath to help the glass break off easier (Fig. 7-4).

Tap the glass if needed. Then place a piece of wood or dowel under the scored line to ready the glass for breaking along the line (Fig. 7-5). The method used to break the glass is shown in Fig. 7-6. Grasp the glass firmly as shown. Push down on the side to be discarded with a quick snapping action. You should get a good clean break and a piece of glass which should fit properly into your frame.

Glass cutting is a very easy job if you do not rush into it. As with any operation of framing, practice will improve your performance. The important part of cutting glass is to use a good sharp cutter.

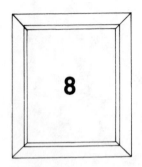

# 8 Assembly

The final assembly of your framing is an important step in that it will protect your work and allow you to hang it properly. The final assembly puts the finishing touch to a job well done. As the cabinet maker puts a back on his cabinet, you should put a back on your framing to protect it from direct and dust. As with any job, hobby or craft, the finishing touch is what makes all the prior work pay off.

## TOOLS AND SUPPLIES

The tools and supplies you will need for the assembly process include a backing board (cardboard), brads, a flat sided hammer, white glue, kraft paper, an awl or ice pick, screw eyes and picture hanging wire. One of the most important things needed for the assembly will be a good clean flat surface to work on. Remember that you have put a lot of work into your framing project up to this point. It is necessary that you give each component as much protection as possible during assembly.

## CARDBOARD BACKING

Providing your work area is ready for assembly, start the work by giving the glass a very thorough cleaning on both sides before inserting it into the frame (Fig. 8-1). After the glass has been properly cleaned, turn the frame face down and insert the glass, which should be a good fit (Fig. 8-2). Upon the glass you will place the matted picture (Fig. 8-3). Next will come the cardboard backing (Fig. 8-4).

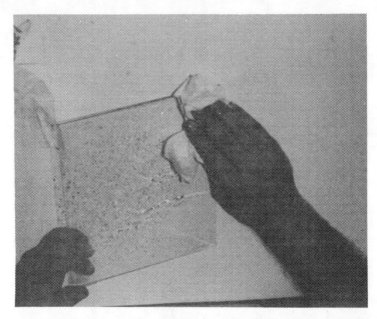

Fig. 8-1. The glass should be cleaned thoroughly before inserting.

Fig. 8-2. Inserting the glass into the frame rabbet.

Fig. 8-3. Place the matted picture upon the glass.

Fig. 8-4. The cardboard backing is placed upon the picture.

The next step is important in that it holds the backing snug against the print and glass. A brad will be inserted in the center of each side into the frame with part of the brad resting on the backing to make it tight. The brads are inserted with a flat-sided hammer (Fig. 8-5). As you insert the brads, push down on the backing to provide a good fit. Now that the two initial brads have been inserted, turn the frame over to be sure the assembly is properly centered. If any adjustments need to be made, now is the time, before the backing is completely fastened. When you are satisfied with the centering of the print, drive brads all around the frame, 3 or 4 inches apart, using the hammer (Fig. 8-6).

## KRAFT PAPER BACKING

With the backing board in place and secure, you are ready to apply the kraft paper backing, which is the final deterrent against the entry of dust. Cut the kraft paper large enough to allow for some overhang. Then moisten the paper with a wrung out damp cloth (Fig. 8-7). Apply glue to the back edge of the frame in the manner shown (Fig. 8-8). Lay the dampened kraft paper over the back of the frame, smoothing it out and pressing it to the glued edge (Fig. 8-9). The paper will need to dry. When it does, it will shrink and

Fig. 8-5. Inserting the brads.

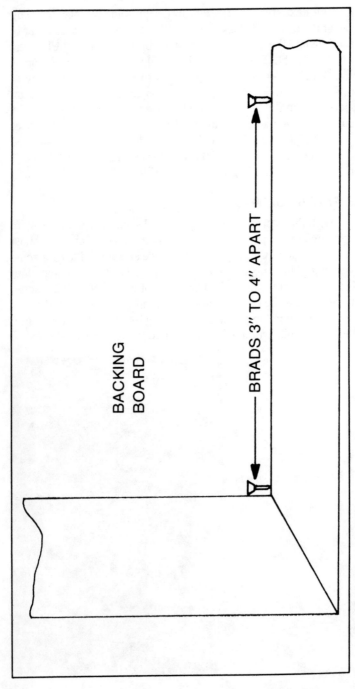

BACKING
BOARD

BRADS 3″ TO 4″ APART

Fig. 8-6. The brads should be spaced 3 or 4 inches apart.

116

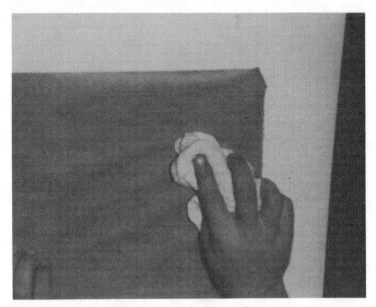

Fig. 8-7. Moisten the kraft paper to make it expand.

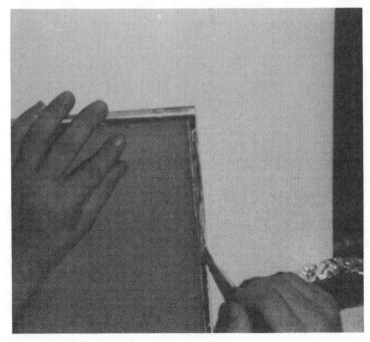

Fig. 8-8. Apply glue to the back of the frame.

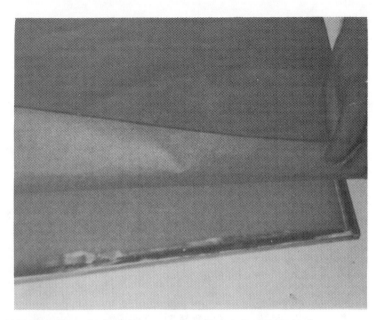

Fig. 8-9. Place the kraft paper over the glued surface of the back.

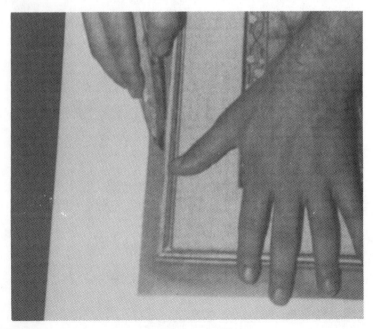

Fig. 8-10. Trim any overhang to finish the backing.

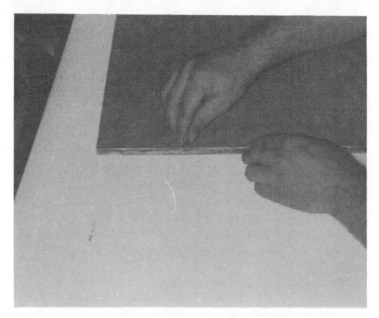

Fig. 8-11. Inserting the screw eyes.

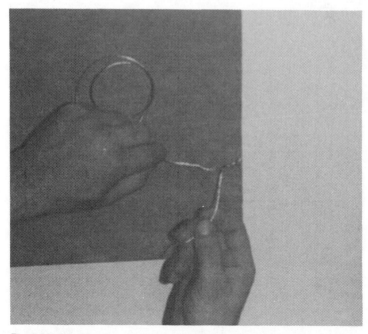

Fig. 8-12. Attaching the wire through the screw eyes.

119

make a tight, dustproof cover. When the paper has dried suffi-
ciently, trim the overhang even with the edge of the frame (Fig.
8-10). Remove any excess glue from the frame with extra fine
sandpaper.

## INSERTING SCREW EYES AND CONNECTING THE WIRE

Your next step is to ready the framing for hanging by inserting
screw eyes into the frame and connecting the wire. On the back of
the frame, make a mark for the screw eyes on both sides one-third
of the way down from the top. When an awl or ice pick, make a
starting hole for the screw eyes in the frame. Insert the screw eyes
as in Fig. 8-11, screwing them in as far as they will go. If the eyes
start turning hard, put the awl through the eye and use this as
method of leverage. Cut the picture wire about 12 inches longer
than the width of the frame. Loop the end of the wire through the
screw eyes two or three times, leaving a loose end about 3 to 4
inches long (Fig. 8-12). Twist the loose end around the wire that
crosses the back of the picture. Proceed to the other side with the
same operation, adjusting the slack of the wire so that it does not
show above the frame. With this completed, you are ready to hang
your picture.

# Framing a Canvas   9

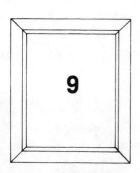

Up to this point the discussion of framing has dealt mainly with framing such mediums as watercolors, pastels, etc., that would require the protection of a glass. If you are an artist, you probably have also worked in oils on a stretched canvas. This chapter will deal with the framing of artwork in that medium. Actually, the framing of a canvas is basic to other framing operations, but there are a few different considerations which need to be mentioned.

## THE LINER

Although a canvas can be framed with just a single outside molding, it is best to incorporate a *liner* much for the same reason you used a mat on prints. The liner is a frame which fits into the outside frame and creates a harmonious break between the outside molding and the canvas (Fig. 9-1). The size or width of the liner is determined much in the same manner as you determined the width of the mat. The liner will range in width of ¼ inch and up.

The liner can take on many different shapes as well as treatments of finishes. The liner is found in flat, rounded or beveled shapes as well as having its total surface carved or an edge treatment, as the liner in Fig. 9-2. The liner can be painted and gilded (a gold treatment on the edge) as in Fig. 9-2 or covered with a fabric as in Fig. 9-3, with either the entire surface being covered or a partial treatment.

Fig. 9-1. A liner is a frame which fits in an outer frame.

Fig. 9-2. A carved edge treatment of a liner.

Fig. 9-3. A liner partially covered with fabric.

## STEP-BY-STEP PROCEDURE

One consideration to be made in framing a canvas is the tolerance you must allow for the fitting of the canvas inside the rabbet of the frame. As mentioned earlier, the tolerance for a

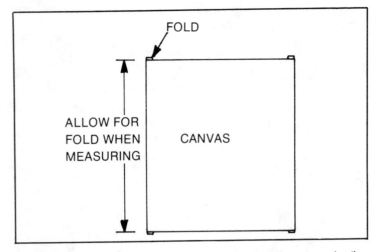

Fig. 9-4. Take the folds of the canvas into consideration when measuring the canvas.

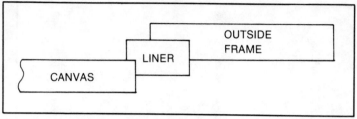

Fig. 9-5. A view of a frame, liner and canvas.

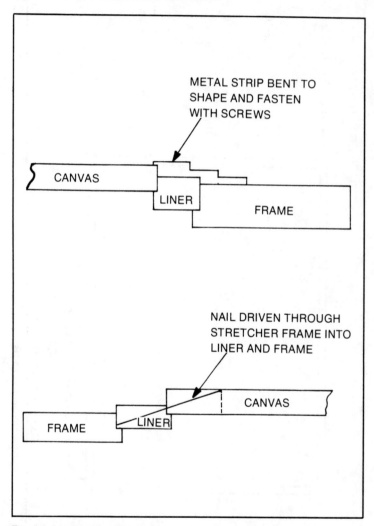

Fig. 9-6. Mounting the canvas.

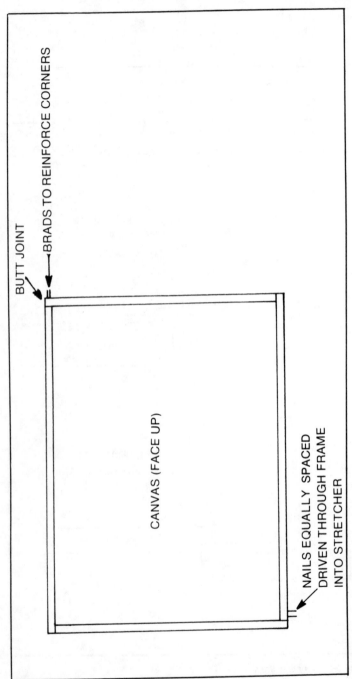

Fig. 9-7. The steps in stripping a canvas.

canvas is usually ¼ inch total to allow for expansion as well as out of square stretcher frames. When you measure your canvas, be sure to take the measurement as in Fig. 9-4, which takes into consideration the folds at the corner of the stretched canvas.

After the measurements are taken and all calculations are made for the frame size, you will cut and join the frame as you did in prior chapters. Once the liner size is established and joined, it will become the basis for the outside frame. As a combination, the total framing will appear as in Fig. 9-5.

Once the two frames are complete, mount the canvas in the inner frame (Fig. 9-6). The next step is to insert your screw eyes and attach the wire as you did for the other assemblies in prior chapters.

## STRIPPING

Another method of framing a canvas is called *stripping* and is exactly what the name implies. In this type of framing a strip which has no rabbet is applied to the outside edge of the painting, with the corners of the molding either being mitered or butted (Fig. 9-7). The molding can either be a plain strip or one which is shaped, and is usually ¼ inch to ½ inch wide by 1½ inches to 2 inches deep.

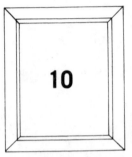

# Making Frames From Used Wood, Barn Wood or Flat Planks

## 10

Another type of frame which has become popular for country or folk art is one which is made from used or barn wood, or flat planks which are distressed. The frame shown in Fig. 10-1 is an example of such a frame. It is made from wide and narrow flats placed one upon the other and distressed with a gouge. If you will recall from Chapter 1, this type of frame is made along the same lines as the platform frame.

### BEGINNING STEPS

To make this type of frame, you will use the same methods as were used in Chapter 4 by creating a rabbet for the picture to fit into. In the following frame the large flat will create the rabbet and a narrow strip will be used as a top molding.

After measuring your picture to be framed, cut your miters as in Fig. 10-2 in the large flats. After the four miters have been cut, you are ready to join the frame members.

### JOINING FRAME MEMBERS

For joining a wide flat, you may not be able to use the regular clamp used in the gluing operation. If the flat is too wide, place the corner in a device as shown in Fig. 10-3. Clamp the corner down with C-clamps until it is dry. After you have completed the wide flat, cut and join the narrow flat which will extend over the inside edge of the large flat about ¼ inch. Completing the small flat, apply

Fig. 10-1. An example of flats used for a frame.

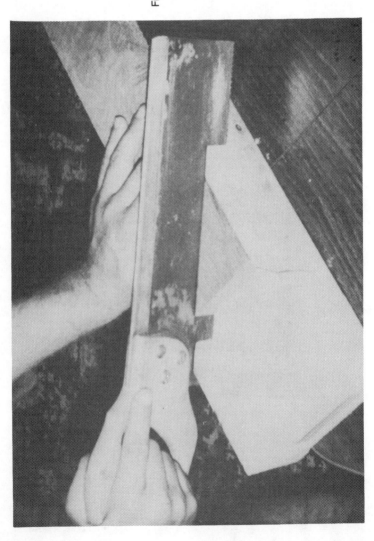

Fig. 10-2. Make the miter cuts.

Fig. 10-3. Joining a wide flat.

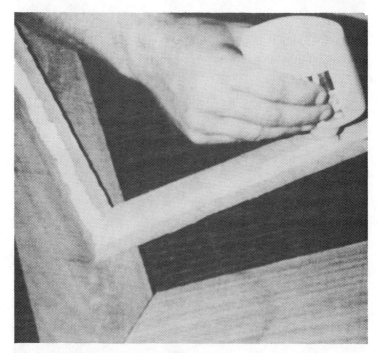

Fig. 10-4. Apply glue to the back side.

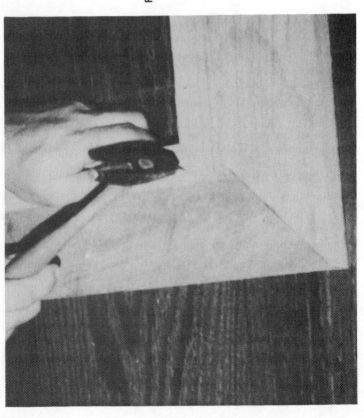

Fig. 10-5. Nail the small flat to the large flat with brads.

Fig. 10-6. The completed frame.

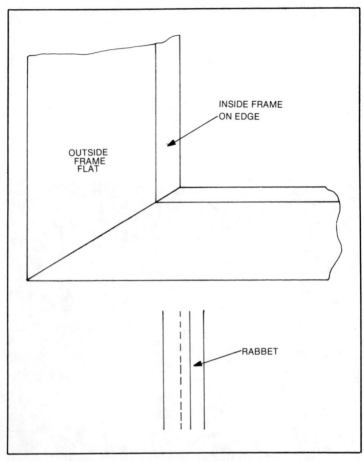

Fig. 10-7. A frame with an inner frame to hold the picture.

glue to the back side (Fig. 10-4). Attach it to the large flat with the use of brads (Fig. 10-5). Your completed frame will appear as in Fig. 10-6.

The method of finishing a frame of this type is usually kept simple. This type of frame seems very popular for the framing of a canvas, and the final assembly should be as you have studied before.

### VARIATIONS

The frame in Fig. 10-7 is made by placing the inner frame on edge. In the frame depicted in Fig. 10-8, flat planks are joined in a

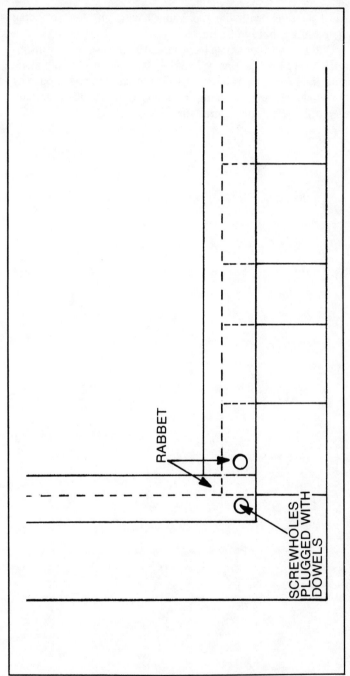

RABBET

SCREWHOLES
PLUGGED WITH
DOWELS

Fig. 10-8. A vertical arrangement of boards for a frame.

135

vertical position, with the top frame having an effect of being doweled to the bottom frame.

Different variations can be achieved by the use of your imagination. There are also many finishes, but you should stay along simple lines such as painted, distressed and stained. You may choose to leave the wood in its raw state. Barn wood is especially pretty when left in its natural state.

# Shadow Box 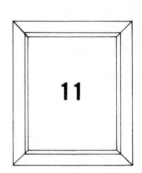 11

The *shadow box* is used to display a three-dimensional object. You may have a group of medals which you are proud of and want to show them off, and there is no better way than that of a shadow box. The shadow box must have enough depth sufficient to create strong and deep shadows. The actual depth of the box is in direct relation to the thickness of the object framed.

## ESTABLISHING RABBET DEPTH

To establish the depth of the rabbet of the frame, you first measure the thickness of the object to be framed. After getting this measurement, remember that you are going to have a space between the glass and the object to create the depth mentioned before. The rabbet depth must also allow for the thickness of the glass, the thickness of the mounting board and the backing board (Fig. 11-1).

The shadow box in Fig. 11-2 is the home of some prized medals from the past. The frame is stained dark walnut and the mounting board is covered with a rich red cloth. To make a shadow box of this type, select and cover the mounting board by gluing the cloth to the board as in Fig. 11-3, which will hold the medals. When the board has been covered, the medals are sewn on with nylon thread; be sure to pierce the mounting board (Fig. 11-4).

## CONSTRUCTION AND ASSEMBLY

Measure and join your frame as you did in prior chapters, using the dimensions of the mounting board to calculate the dimen-

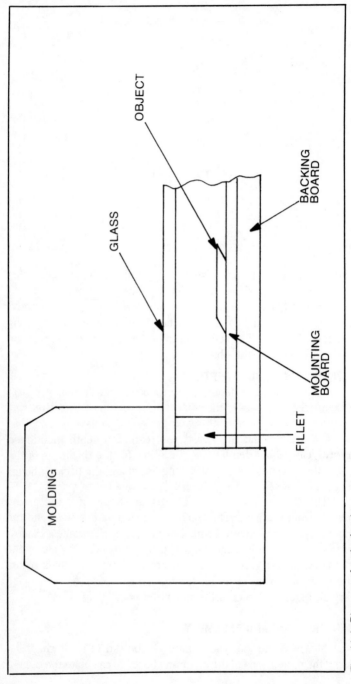

Fig. 11-1. Diagram of a shadow box.

Fig. 11-2. A finished shadow box.

Fig. 11-3. The cloth is glued to the mounting board.

Fig. 11-4. Medals are sewn on with nylon thread.

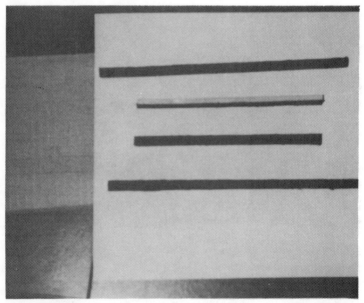

Fig. 11-5. Fillets are needed to allow space between the glass and the mounting board.

sions of your frame. After the frame has been assembled and finished, you will need to make four *fillets* which are covered with the same material as the mounting board and then glued to the side of the frame (Fig. 11-5). The fillets will hold the glass in place against the frame rabbet and form a rabbet for the mounting board. The fillets should be no wider than the rabbet of the frame. After cleaning and placing the glass in the frame and gluing the fillets in place, you are ready to insert the mounting board and make your final assembly (Figs. 11-6 and 11-7).

With the fillets glued in place, leave the frame face down and insert the mounting board (Fig. 11-8). Then place the backing board next to the mounting board (Fig. 11-9). Press down on the backing board while placing a brad in the center of each side of the frame (Fig. 11-10). Then flip the frame over to check for proper alignment of the framing before completely fastening the back in place. If no adjustments are necessary, proceed to fasten the back by placing brads 3 to 4 inches apart around the back (Fig. 11-11).

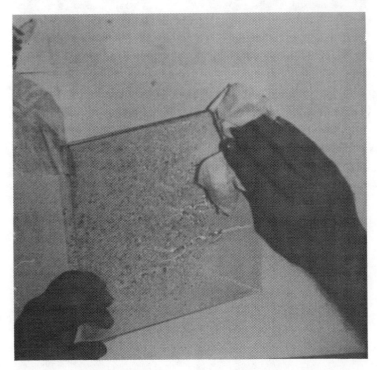

Fig. 11-6. Cleaning the glass.

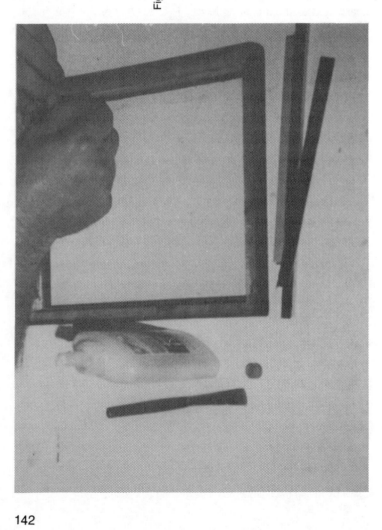

Fig. 11-7. Glue the fillets to the frame.

Fig. 11-8. Insert the mounting board.

Fig. 11-9. Insert the backing board next to the mounting board.

Fig. 11-10. Drive a brad in the center of two sides.

Fig. 11-11. Place the brads 3 or 4 inches apart.

Fig. 11-12. Apply glue to the back of the frame.

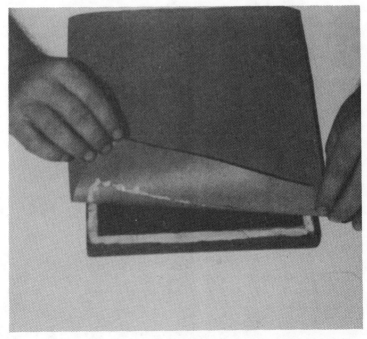

Fig. 11-13. Dampen the kraft paper to make it expand, and place it on the back.

Fig. 11-14. Trim any excess paper when it is dry.

Fig. 11-15. Attach screw eyes.

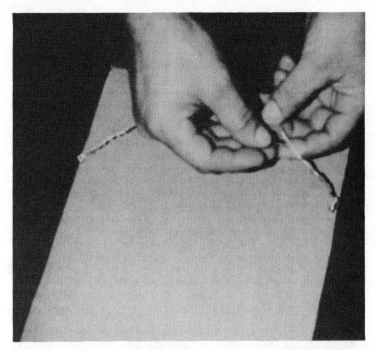

Fig. 11-16. When the wire is fastened, the shadow box is ready for hanging.

With the back fastened down, apply the glue to the frame (Fig. 11-12). Place the dampened kraft paper onto the back (Fig. 11-13). Trim around the edge which the paper is dry (Fig. 11-14). Next mark the spots for the screw eyes and insert as in Fig. 11-15. Attach the wire, and your shadow box is ready for hanging (Fig. 11-16).

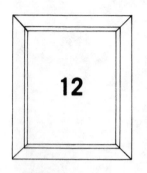

# Making Your Own Moldings

**12**

This chapter will provide you with the know-how to produce moldings of your own design from raw wood. The reasons why you may wish to make your own moldings could be many. The first thought is the pure economics of doing it. If you have the power tools and equipment necessary to perform the molding operations, it would be wise to use them. If you are just beginning in this craft, I would suggest you postpone such a large purchase until you are sure that you enjoy or could profit from the craft of framing. Another reason for making the moldings is the wood you may want to use. Since choice hardwoods are used for a waxed finish, you will find it much cheaper to produce the molding than to buy. Whatever the reason you have for making your moldings, the following should help in getting you started or help you to decide if it is something you wish to tackle.

## THE MOLDING HEAD SET

If you choose to make your own moldings, you will need a *radial arm saw*, or a table saw, and a *molding head set*. The molding head set fits onto the saw in the same manner as the blade does and gives you a wide range of single shapes which each knife is used alone (Fig. 12-1). In Fig. 12-2 you can see the many different profiles of the knives in the particular molding set of Fig. 12-1.

### Producing Profiles

The interesting part of the molding set is that the knives can be used in sequence and at different angles to produce an array of profiles. One example of the operation is shown in Fig. 12-3. There are many more profiles to be made by simple experimentation.

To plot your different profiles, start by cutting a piece of poster board to the size of the raw lumber you will be using. Trace the intended knife outline as shown (Fig. 12-4). As seen in each step, the profile progresses as each knife is positioned on the template. After you get your template complete, cut the profile out with scissors, being sure to cut exactly. The profile you now have can be transferred to the end of the workpiece to aid in setting the knives for each cut (Fig. 12-5). If you like the profile you produce, be sure to keep the template along with a record of the knives used and their sequence.

With any tool such as the molding set, the important thing is that you use sharp knives to make your cuts. Also, use the proper guides and guards. Always exercise safety when you are using power tools. One of the first accessories you may want to make for use with the molding set is a push stick, which will keep your fingers away from the rotating knives (Fig. 12-6).

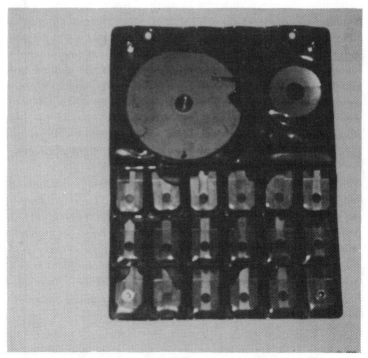

Fig. 12-1. A molding set for use with the table or radial saw.

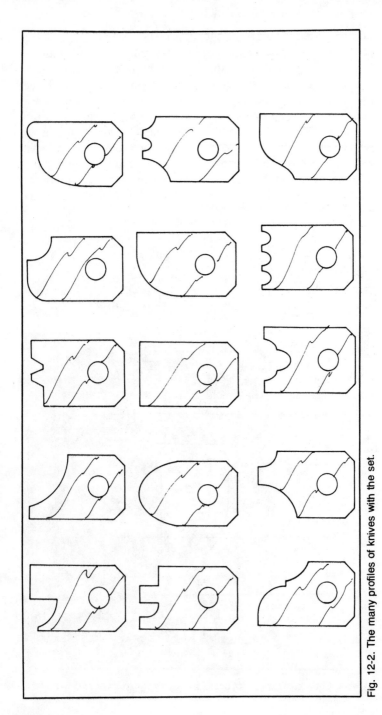

Fig. 12-2. The many profiles of knives with the set.

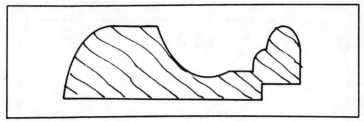

Fig. 12-3. A molding profile.

## Table Saw Setup

The molding set can be used with either the table or radial saw, and you will need to make some special setups for the molding set's use. To use the molding head with the table saw, you will need a cutout in the fence for the molding head to clear. To make the fence, use two 1-inch boards and clamp or bolt them to the fence already provided with your saw (Fig. 12-7). A molding insert must also be used with the molding head to allow for the proper clearance of the set. The molding set will attach to your saw arbor in the same manner as the saw blade, but follow the instructions provided with the molding set for attachment.

Your molding operation with the table saw is much like feeding a workpiece into a saw blade. Always use the fence as a guide and hold the piece being molded firmly during the operation.

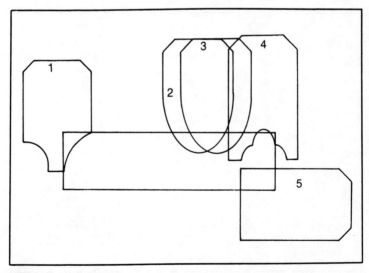

Fig. 12-4. Cut a piece of poster board the size of raw lumber and trace the intended knife outline.

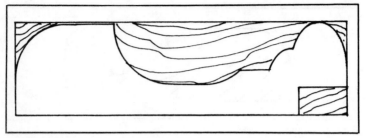

Fig. 12-5. Transfer the profile to the end of the workpiece.

Always use a push stick if your fingers must pass close to the knives.

## STRIP MOLDING

*Strip molding* may also be made with the molding set on the table saw. There are two ways of achieving the strip molding. One way is to edge mold a wide strip and cut the molding off by ripping on the saw. If thin stock is to be molded, a special setup, called a stripping guide, must be used (Fig. 12-8). The guide must be grooved to the exact size of the thin stock used, and a cover is made as shown in Fig. 12-8 with a cutout to allow for the knives to make their cut. The guide is clamped to the fence. The thin stock is molded by feeding it through the knives.

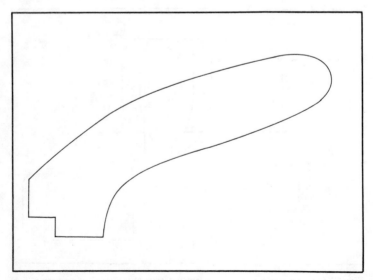

Fig. 12-6. A push stick will aid in molding.

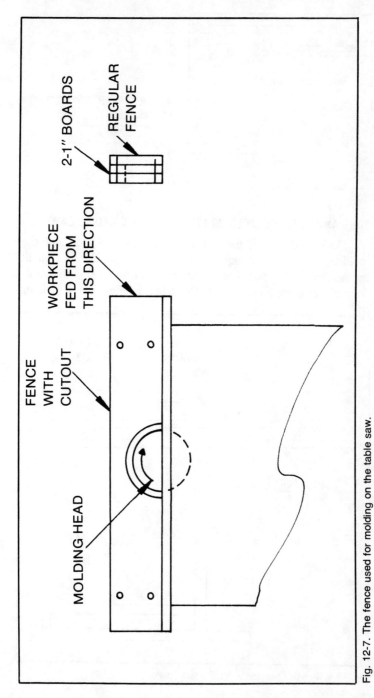

REGULAR FENCE

2-1" BOARDS

WORKPIECE FED FROM THIS DIRECTION

FENCE WITH CUTOUT

MOLDING HEAD

Fig. 12-7. The fence used for molding on the table saw.

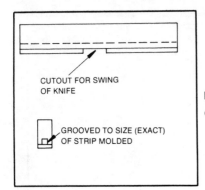

CUTOUT FOR SWING OF KNIFE

GROOVED TO SIZE (EXACT) OF STRIP MOLDED

Fig. 12-8. A stripping guide is used on the table saw.

## EDGE AND SURFACE MOLDING SETUPS ON THE RADIAL SAW

As stated earlier, the radial saw can also be used with the molding set for making your own moldings. The molding set will fit on the saw just as the blade does and must be used with guards during the molding operations. For edge molding, use a molding

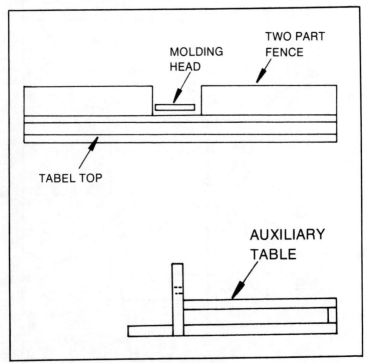

MOLDING HEAD

TWO PART FENCE

TABEL TOP

AUXILIARY TABLE

Fig. 12-9. The two part fence for the radial saw.

154

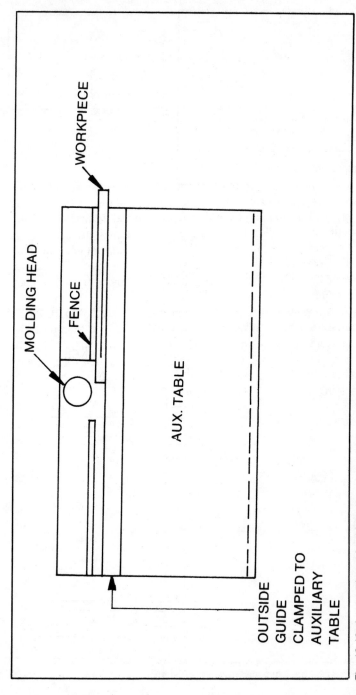

MOLDING HEAD

WORKPIECE

FENCE

AUX. TABLE

OUTSIDE
GUIDE
CLAMPED TO
AUXILIARY
TABLE

Fig. 12-10. An outside guide aids in the control of the workpiece.

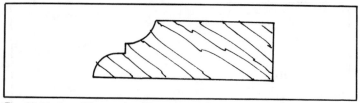

Fig. 12-11. A molding made with a single cut.

head guard. For surface molding, you can use the regular guard supplied with your saw.

To produce edge moldings on the radial saw you will need a special setup, which is a two part fence to allow for the molding head, and an auxiliary table (Fig. 12-9). To make an edge molding, set the fence to allow for the swing of the head and cutters. Another guide may be attached to the table to allow a steadier job of molding and is very useful if short pieces are being molded (Fig. 12-10). Never hesitate to use a push stick during any operation to keep your fingers clear of the molding knives.

After the pattern you wish to make has been chosen, place the knife in the head, adjust the height and fence, and then push the material toward the knife, as with a ripping operation (Fig. 12-10). The molding you produce in a single cut such as this will appear as in Fig. 12-11, and this single shape alone could be used for a frame molding.

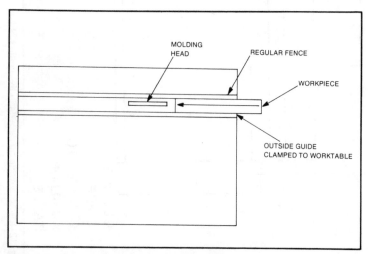

Fig. 12-12. The setup used for surface molding.

For surface molding the setup is made as in Fig. 12-12, with the regular guard used on the saw. You will not need the auxiliary table for surface molding, but it is still best to use the outside guide as shown for better control of the workpiece. This gives you a basic idea of what can be done with a molding set in relation to making picture frame molding. The molding set is a fine asset to any home workshop and is a wise purchase if power tools fit into your budget.

# Index

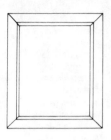

Edited by Robert E. Ostrander